Akiane—
My Dream Is Bigger Than I

Memories of Tomorrow

Copyright © 2006 Akiane Kramarik

ISBN 10: 0-9778697-0-9
ISBN 13: 978-0-9778697-0-1
SAN 850-3745

All rights reserved. No part of this book may be reproduced or transmitted in any form or by any means, electronic or mechanical, including photocopying, recording, or by information storage and retrieval systems, without the written permission of the publisher, except by a reviewer who may quote brief passages in a review.

Published by
Artakiane LLC
P.O. Box 2860
Post Falls Idaho 83877
800-318-0947

To purchase autographed books by Akiane,
to purchase her original paintings or limited edition prints on canvas,
or to write to her, please E-mail Akiane Studio Gallery at:
love@artakiane.com

To find out about Akiane's appearances on television, radio, art shows, art auctions, conferences, fund-raising and other events, please visit her web site:
www.artakiane.com

CREDITS:

Cover design: Ryan Feasel, BookMasters, Inc.

Front cover painting: Akiane Kramarik

Text Design: Kristen Butler, BookMasters, Inc.

Back cover photo: Jay Ellis, Ellis studios

Other photos: Mark, Delfini and Foreli Kramarik, Emily Ward,
Johana Koeb, Jay Ellis, Natalie Camino, Sean Watson and Chris Gibbs

Assistance in translation, text design, proof-reading and editing: Foreli Kramarik

Proof-reading and editing:
Linda Erickson, Victoria Potts, Chad Klinger and Laurie Lamon

Proof-reading: Michelle Smith

Advisory support: Roger Jellinek, Sandy Ross, Michael Lloyd
and Jeanlu Kramarik

Library of Congress Control Number: 2006901769

Printed in the United States of America

Akiane—
My Dream Is Bigger Than I
Memories of Tomorrow

Akiane Kramarik

Artakiane.LLC
www.artakiane.com

What They Say About Akiane:

"Akiane . . . is a prodigy!"
World News Tonight, ABC

"I am blown away!"
Montel Williams, Montel Williams Show, CBS

"What an amazing and talented young girl!!!"
Craig Ferguson, Late Late Show

". . . Nothing has prepared us for Akiane!.."
Lou Dobbs, Lou Dobbs Tonight, CNN

"Wow, what an inspiration!"
Wayne Brady, The Wayne Brady show

"Akiane's work is a miracle. It must come from God."
**Jurij Sizenov Nikolaevich, Shabolovka/
Russian television/radio mega network**

". . . Akiane is . . . incredible . . ."
Robert Schuler, Hour Of Power/Crystal Cathedral

*"Wow! Wow! We want to warn you—
her inspired poetry is very deep!"*
WavFile TV program CJIL/Miracle Channel/Canada

". . . What a divine anointing!"
Extreme Prophetic TV program CJIL/Miracle Channel/Canada

". . . Akiane is a sign of the times . . ."
Lifeline TV program CJIL/Miracle Channel/Canada

"To say that Akiane has extraordinary talent is a gross understatement. She is a young genius and a spiritual young lady with an amazing gift who is changing the lives of all who have come in contact with her."
Fox Magazine/Fox News

"... This youngster ... has been touched ..."
J.C. and Friends, Gannet television/CBS

"Akiane is connected with the Divine Source that we all aspire to connect with. Her ... poetry provides us with the memories and link to that place of wholeness from which we come from and seek to return to ..."
Kent Romney, filmmaker, co-producer/director—"Indigo Evolution"

"Divine gift ..."
BBC Russian

"Akiane's story is unusual ... and its uniqueness reflects God's ... existence."
Ieva magazine/Lithuania

"... The whole world cannot be indifferent to this rare talent. Angelic face, Akiane amazes everyone with her creations ..."
Amerikos Lietuvis

"... Poetry is her heart and soul ..."
Fine Arts Phenom/The Press newspaper/Idaho

"... Akiane's work is fabulous!"
Weekly Reader magazine

"... Beyond her years ..."
Southwest Outlook newspaper

"As gifted as she is in art and literature,
Akiane's greatest gift is her faith."
The Heartland Gatekeeper newspaper/Omaha

"... Divinely talented..."
The Sun magazine

"... an amazing gift..."
Today's Christian magazine

"... Incredible... poetry..."
Rainbow News/New Zealand

"... God has given Akiane an amazing gift."
Shine newspaper

"... Akiane is dazzling everyone with her poetry...
all meaningful and symbolic."
Strokes of Genius/Spokesman Review newspaper/Washington

"Without any argument or doubt, Akiane is great!"
Victor Depuev, the Academy of Sciences of Russia, Moscow

"Akiane's innocence, her vision, and compassion all come
through in her... poetry. I believe this young and gifted
child is destined to leave her mark in the world..."
**Edward Solomon, Co-founder and Director of the International
Museum of 21st Century Art (TIMOTCA), Art Beyond Borders**

"Akiane's striking poetry are windows into the soul of her
subjects reaching a depth far beyond her years."
Victoria Nesnick, Ph.D., President, founder/Kids Hall of Fame

"Akiane's words are so amazing and powerful.
They literally capture the revelatory truth and essence!"
**Paul Keith Davis, author, public speaker, and
co-founder/White Dove Ministries**

"... As I read Akiane's poetry, it's very
clear to me that God is with us..."
**Michael Lloyd, an award winning music
producer, composer and poet**

"Akiane is an absolute artistic prodigy. Her poetry is out of this world. I can't wait to see the translations in many languages."
**Marina Koledinsteva, Ph.D., professor,
poet, inventor, University of Missouri**

"... A rare diamond! Akiane's gift is invaluable and long awaited."
**Michael Ward, M.ED., Psychotherapist
Emily Ward, CEO and president Le Triomphe,Inc.Intl.**

"... Advanced and beautiful works!.. Akiane's spirituality is so uncommon for a child her age."
Renee and Brent Caudil, M.D.

"Akiane's powerful poetry explains God in such a mystic and entrancing manner that it makes me want to read more."
Adora Svitak, eight-year-old author "Flying Fingers"

"... Akiane's genius is her ability to absorb the world around her and translate exactly what she sees in perfect form."
**Rick Hancock, President/CEO, ABI,
International Art Dealer and Publisher**

"Akiane is all at once a brilliant blend of adult and child weaving profound wisdom with pure innocence in every word she writes and every stroke she paints."
**Freddie Ravel, #1 Recording Artist,
Composer, Author and Speaker**

"Akiane's poetry ... is a timeless and exquisite whisper of grace! Akiane is beyond blessed!"
**Chris Haase, curator, president/the board of directors,
The Museum Of Religious Arts, Iowa**

"Reading Akiane's poetry was like a day with William Blake or Emily Dickinson. What a high energy, powerfully evocative, thought-provoking and moving poetry."
**Chad Klinger, author "It's How You Play
The Game—An Approach To Poetry."**

"Akiane is a literary phenomenon in the history of poetic art. I doubt that has ever been a literary child genius of such maturity, lyrical virtuosity, and spiritual transcendence. Her rarest gift will be engraved forever in the history pages of the world's literature. I see the cosmic hope and meaning of life in her wisdom-saturated imagery that reminds me of quantum physics. I am speechless. I am an old man in tears. And I bow down to her miraculous genius. Thanks to Akiane, I am no longer an atheist!"
Vladislovas Blinstubas, celebrated Lithuanian poet

"It seems that these expressions are not those of a young girl, but of a mature poet whose aphoristic and enigmatic thinking come to her instantly. Hers is definitely a philosophical poetry, and our Earthly literature can be so proud of this 'wunderkind'."
Alfred Guschius, distinguished literary critic and poet

"I have never encountered such talent for anyone so young. The images of Akiane's poetry are astonishingly mature and original, fearless, deep, and mysteriously powerful. Yet Akiane herself remains an unpretentious, unselfconscious, delightfully unaffected and playful girl!"
**Roger Jellinek, literary agent, editor,
speaker/International Writers' conference**

"Akiane is treasure. A poised, engaged, and beautiful young person with hard-to-comprehend talents. Her poetry and paintings are gifts to all of us."
**Emory Miller, Senior Vice President for
Government Affairs/Robbins Gioia LLC**

Dedication

I dedicate this book to my family. Their guidance, support and encouragement unwrapped the gifts I had received.

My gratitude goes to my mother who listened to me patiently while I shared my creations with her. My deepest respect goes to my dad and my three brothers who were always supportive in my search for truth. My prayers go to different families whose lives I was privileged to see in my visions. And my love goes to all the children who depend on our promises . . .

_____Akiane__

Contents

Introduction   xxv

Forward   xxix

Part 1   Age 7   1

    The Calluses 2
    The Bells 3
    The Sprouting Grass 4
    The Divorce Of Resurrection 5
    A Loaf Of Bread 6
    Clay 7
    So Much Of You 8
    All Too Fast 9
    Yes, I Am Weak 10
    I AM 11
    A Dove 12
    In Coals 13
    Scars 14
    My Garden 15
    ..S..h..a..t..t..e..r..e..d.. 16
    Between Shores 17
    The Lantern 18
    The Birdfeeder 19
    The Knocks 20
    Life 21
    Today 22
    The Nightingales 23
    The Wrinkles 24
    The Butterflies 25
    A Wedding 26
    How Much Is It Worth? 27
    Planting The Paradise 28

	The Color Of A Smile	29
	The Lips Of War	30
	The Ark	31
	The Robe	32
	In An Unobstructed View	33
	The Departure	34
	The Trap	35
	Venom	36
Part II	**Age 8**	**37**
	The Lighthouse	38
	The Waiting	39
	The Strength	40
	The Fingerprints	41
	Under A Cast	42
	Gratitude	43
	Invitation To Love	44
	Trespassed	45
	Shot Swans	46
	The Grand Piano	47
	He Had To Hope	48
	Unborn Child	49
	The Chosen Echo	50
	The Clearest Reality	51
	A Present For My Father	52
	Off The Rail	53
	Tracked Down	54
	This Was The Time	55
	Clay Cradle	56
	Letters	57
	Your Candles Are Soft	58
	From The Fenced Lands	59
	I Love You	60
	One Wave	61
	The Day I Was Born	62
	Free Will	63
	The Last White Hair	64
	The Paper Boat	65

The Cloak 66
The Last Lullaby 67
The Relief 68
The Shapelessness 69
I Need Only You 70
The Old Age 71
The Stolen Painting 72
Wings Over Me 73
The Pilgrim 74
The Waves 75
Weakness Below A Cast 76

Part III   Age 9   77

Spiritual Knowledge 78
The Price Of Feeling 79
Consciousness Of Giving 80
Heart-strings 81
When We Lift The Shell 82
A Soldier 83
All Color Eyes 84
What Color Am I? 85
During A Race 86
Florescent Lives 87
I Lean Against Love 88
In The Soil 89
Next Breeze Is Free 90
Eternity Thumbnail 91
Staining The Rust 92
Dried Tears Never Reach A Rainbow 93
Too Far Away 94
Thunderstorms 95
A Mystery 96
Too Blurry 97
White Kisses 98
Never Hitting The Ground 99
You Can Take Everything I Have 100
Adolescence 101
Almost 102

It Is Your Eyes I Am Looking For *103*
Barefoot *104*
Homeward Trapped *105*
Dizzy *106*
Thirst Follows Even Ice *107*
Whose Imagination? *108*
The Seeking *109*
By Faith *110*
The Ice Skater *112*
New Generation *113*
Only A Moment *114*
The Splinters *115*
Not One Of Us *116*
Up Or Down *117*
In The Captivity Of A Mask *118*
A Perfect Score *119*

Part IV Age 10   121

A Snowflake *122*
The Extraction Of Inspiration *123*
A Sign *124*
Endangered *125*
By The Light *126*
Hanging Upside Down *127*
This Is My Life *128*
The Perfection *129*
The Sand Of Trying *130*
All The Crossroads *131*
Promises And Secrets *132*
Between The Wrinkles Of The Edge *133*
Brittle *134*
A Double-Sided Sword *135*
A Bent Horizon *136*
Masquerade *137*
The Eclipse Of Darkness *138*

Contents

Existence	*139*
The Released Arrow	*140*
Where Do I Turn?	*141*
It Must Be Felt	*142*
Across The Universe	*143*
Life Of Climbing	*144*
The Hypothermic Love	*145*
Beyond The Exceptions	*146*
Forgiveness	*147*
Life Of Frames And Circles	*148*
One Plant At A Time	*149*
With Dust	*150*
Portrait Of Chances	*151*
Here I Am	*152*
An Aftertaste	*153*
The Infinity Of Beginning	*154*
Confidential	*155*
A Kiss	*156*
I Am Yours	*157*
The Flame Of The Time	*158*
Last Beat	*159*
Adam And Eve	*160*
On The Edge Of A Bridge	*161*
Not By Accident	*162*
In The Rain	*163*
In The Middle	*164*
The Race Track	*165*
Confused	*166*
On The Cloud Stage	*167*
Panoramic View	*168*
Celestial Warmth	*169*
Mother Loaf	*170*
The Tempo Of The Seasons	*171*
Ports	*172*
Atrophy	*173*
Prepared	*174*
Scabs Of Knowledge	*175*

Akiane

Part V Age 11   177

Just One Of You *178*
Down A Mudslide *179*
Detached *180*
Definition *181*
Between My Shoulders *182*
Invitation To The Scars *183*
Licking Your Wounds *184*
Outside Themselves *185*
Don't Cross Life *186*
The Fence *187*
In The Distance *188*
The Promise *189*
When You Leave *190*
Your Eyes Over Mine *191*
The Eternal Terms *192*
Among The Noble Hearts *193*
A Foursquare *194*
Inside Out *195*
A Double Life *196*
You Have Been Here Before *197*
Cannot Keep Track *198*
Before The Shutdown *199*
A Pair Of Rainbows *200*
An Ambush *201*
A Battlefield In Stunned Eyes *202*
The Missing Link *203*
The Divine Wrinkle *204*
The Lies *205*
I Cannot *206*
Mistakenly Mistaken *207*
Profile Of Landscape *208*
Without Me *209*
The Heart-Express *210*
A Fractured Game *211*
The Memories Of Tomorrow *212*
Return Our Hearing Eyes *213*
In The End *214*

    All Of You *215*
    Supreme Sanctuary *216*
    Delicate Reflection *218*
    Not Yet *219*
    My Dream Is Bigger Than I *220*
    Love *221*

Part VI–Reflections   Ages 7–11   223

    Connection *224*
    Beliefs *224*
    Refused Defense *225*
    Childhood *225*
    The Provider *226*
    The Glued Friendship *226*
    Inside My Shell *227*
    Passing Sweetness *227*
    A Contest *228*
    The Drought *228*
    The Irony *229*
    Too Anxious *229*
    Depression *230*
    Taxes *230*
    The Intruder *231*
    Entrapment *231*
    Hope *232*
    Emptied *232*
    The Phenomenon *233*
    The Fight *233*
    Blocked Imagination *234*
    Measuring *234*
    The Riddle *235*
    Gossip *235*
    Tranquility *236*
    The Meaning of Life *236*
    The Rest *237*
    The Surgery *237*
    Division *238*
    Breathing *238*

Competitive	239
Restrained	239
Self-exaltation	240
Rules	240
Still The Truth	241
Infection	241
Vanity	242
Checkmate	242
Flattery	243
Justice	243
Jealousy	244
Fame	244
Sharing	245
Purity	245
Tragedies	246
Permission	246
Affection	247
Distraction	247
Fired	248
Lack Of Air	248
Gauge	249
Doubt	249
Perfection	250
A Title	250
Offspring	251
Fuel	251
Solution	252
Unread	252
Transgression	253
The Distress	253
Boredom	254
Doubt	254
Just Because	255
Life Extension	255
Immature	256
Foreknowledge	256
Unfamiliar	257
Those That Follow	257

Contents

Oblivious	258
Thrown Out	258
A Farmer	259
Dumped	259
Mediocrity	260
Rehearsal	260
For Life	261
A Ripple Effect	261
Gems	262
Effort	262
Knowing The Unknown	263
Missing	263
Dispositions	264
Help	264
Moved	265
Mission	265
The Formula	266
Anger	266
The Spotlight	267
Argument	267
Dry Waiting	268
Who You Are	268
The Virus	269
The Same	269
Source	270
Teaching	270
A Man's Love	271
Building	271
A Chance	272
Load	272
Friendship	273
Injection	273
The Statue	274
Temptations	274
The Cleansing	275
The Persuasion	275
The Circle	276
Cause And Effect	276

Disorganized Help	277
The Influence	277
A Legal Heart	278
The Bridge	278
Overindulgence	279
Useless	279
Envy	280
The Theft	280
Amnesia	281
The Measurements	281
The Joined Roots	282
Patience	282
The Silent Mask	283
The Bribe	283
Levitation	284
The Contentment	284
The Competition	285
Emptiness	285
The Attachment	286
Above The Daring Eyes	286
Except For Love	287
The Prisoner	287
The Sailor	288
The Cure	288
The Forbidden Race	289
No Separation	289
Mutating Hearts	290
Terrestrial Love	290
The Exchanged	291
The Eyes Of Love	291
Opera	292
Indecision	292
In The Beginning	293
Without Any Influence	293
At The Hospital	294
Evolution	294
No Room	295
The Homeless	295

The Recollections *296*
The Stain *296*
Irresistible *297*
The Slave *297*
Captive Audience *298*
The Ultimate Betrayal *298*
Executive Decision *299*
The Inspection *299*
Disconnected *300*
Recollection With An Attitude *300*
A Short Acquaintance *301*
Apathy *301*
Thirst *302*
Paupers *302*
Invasion *303*
A Reminder *303*
A Distraction *304*
Birds Of Prey *304*
The Search *305*
Potential For Darkness *305*
Relationships *306*
The Truth *306*
Between The Sky Scrapers *307*
The Trigger *307*
The Reservation *308*
Compassion *308*
Panoramic Imagination *309*
Cursed *309*
Independence *310*
The Fear *310*
The Fences *311*
One Breath At A Time *311*
The Insanity Circle *312*

Part VII   The Photo Album   **313**

Akiane

The third of four children, Akiane was never exposed to spiritual matters. Unexpectedly, at the age of four, she began sharing her detailed visions about God and events on earth. Soon after, she began drawing and painting stunning portraits.

When Akiane started writing poetry a few years later, the source for the wisdom of her writings was a complete mystery.

As soon as the news reached the media, numerous international television and radio shows, documentaries, magazines and newspapers featured Akiane, including the Oprah Winfrey Show, Good Morning America, World News Tonight/ABC, The Montel Williams Show, Fox Magazine/Fox News, Lou Dobbs Show/CNN, Late Late Show, Wayne Brady Show, Hour of Power/Crystal Cathedral, Lifeline and Extreme Prophetic (Miracle Channel, Canada), Indigo Evolution, Bob&Sheri Show, Drew Mariani show, Time Magazine, Today's Christian magazine and hundreds others.

Akiane was inducted into The Kids' Hall Of Fame and was considered by many the youngest binary child genius in recorded history, for both poetry and realist art.

Yet Akiane has remained innocently unaffected while embarking upon the mission of sharing God's love with the world.

The following is a collection of Akiane's dreams, visions, poetry, aphorisms and philosophical reflections written from the age of seven through eleven.

Her complete biography, along with reproductions of her art, accompanied by poetry, is included in her first book, published by Thomas Nelson—*Akiane: Her Life, Her Art, Her Poetry.*

Introduction

"My Dream Is Bigger Than I" is the book long awaited. For those who have had a privilege to observe Akiane's creativity more intimately, it is nothing short of a miracle, not only because of its substance, but also because of its journey.

Looking back at Akiane's spiritual life there were many unusual manifestations which preceded the beginning of her writings, however, no other event had impacted her family as much as an inexplicable phenomenon witnessed one rainy spring day by so many different people when she was five and a half years old. Akiane simply disappeared . . .

Because of a suspected kidnapping the family estate and close neighborhoods were flooded with policemen, state troopers, patrol-officers, highway officials and neighbors looking for Akiane. Hundreds of vehicles in their small town were stopped for inspection, and the petite girl's photographs were quickly distributed throughout all dispatches.

Then, after many long hours, out of nowhere, there was Akiane, right by the windows in the interior corridor of her house appearing in the midst of numerous eye-witnesses.

"I was with God. There is much work to do. You won't understand this, but you had to experience this event." She consoled her parents and reported exactly what had been going on as though she'd watched the whole scene from above. It was the only physical mystery publicly recorded, and this was the day that moved her formerly faithless family towards acceptance of her unique mission. It was also the day discussed the least, but remembered the most . . .

Throughout this short, yet intense spiritual journey, Akiane was suddenly inspired to write. It started around the time Akiane was seven and a half years old, even though reading, listening to stories or watching theatrical performances rarely intrigued her. And even though at that time there were no friends or acquaintances, no radio or television, and no extended family or long life experiences to lean on for meaningful stories.

Probably the strangest aspect of Akiane's encounter with writing is that she was hardly ever enthusiastic about it, maybe because she easily forgot the full meaning of most reflections, maybe because she could not distinguish her own reactions to life from God's actions, maybe because the philosophy was too deep and too serious for her. Or perhaps it was because she did not want to be distracted from other more appealing pursuits. What Akiane found eventually was that writing about relationships, spiritual battlegrounds and eternal missions was not only her own journey through time and purpose—it was a journey of many. And it had to be shared.

During this poetic journey that spanned four years, Akiane typically seemed bewildered while at the same time giving an impression of both a peaceful vessel filled up with wisdom and an excited messenger trying to remember the prophetic instructions.

The inspired messages came to her in the form of ideas, figures, colors, sounds, vibrations, puzzles, symbols, codes and moving images that were conceived effortlessly in four languages Akiane communicated and then later translated. Yet she was never able to express most of them, because of inability to convert multi-dimensional revelations and sensory perceptions into simple words. In almost all instances she could not understand the full meaning of the insights. However, deep down, she knew they had to be written down anyway.

To her, poetry soon began resembling a multi-dimensional sculpture of a riddle full of events, melodies and impressions, which invited each of us to take part in sculpting and solving its meaning on our own. Whenever she wrote from the first person she usually described others, therefore, according to Akiane, only a few stories were autobiographical, and the messages involved a reader to figure out who "I" and "YOU" were in each page. In other words, a reader was invited along with the author to discern which stories were divine revelations, which stories described emotions of different personalities, and which stories illustrated her own interpretation of life.

When it came to inspiration, Akiane seemed to require no special preparation in order to create. The brilliant imagery was always circulating in her head along with thoughts average for her age. But no one knew when or how they would emerge. During dictation she took certain elements from her immediate surroundings and created powerful messages about distant events, painting their landscape layer by layer like an artist. During the revising, however, she turned into a perceptive sculptor, chiseling the poetic gems out of the plain bulk. The poem was usually surrounded by what Akiane called "the warm-ups" and "cool-downs"—so different from the profound interior message. Akiane would experience an instantaneous recognition of the need to remove the unneeded mass of extraneous language in order to see the final linguistic sculpture. Just as the sculptor chiseling a stone or a diamond is never able to add, but only carefully remove, Akiane was able to discard the excess through inspiration. Only for the final presentation would she add a finishing polish and a glaze of certain lyrical nuances.

Yet in numerous other poetic expressions there were neither her typical warm-ups, nor cool-downs. The poems were fully conceived, apart from the format and punctuation; the rhyme appeared only wherever it appeared naturally or spontaneously. When the poem was created in Lithuanian, Russian or sign language, for instance, the rhyme would not exist, but as soon as it was translated into English, rhyme and unique sound syncopation surfaced. Or the other way around. Occasionally, Akiane switched the rhyming words around for more melodious effect, but in general, she disliked thinking or talking about her writings, especially the rhyme, which to her was unnecessary unless it was already present. During the editing, she made the point that if she could not find a missing rhyme in a text within a few seconds, the poem was meant to remain without it.

"Well, God speaks in rhyme, and he did show me the scroll of light to memorize His wisdom, but since He thinks without any effort, perhaps I do not need to put any effort into my poems, either." And so it was, that writing to her became effortless, even though, at times, the images disturbed her with their vivid emotional graphics of despair, unbelief, struggles, desires, and future of people she had never personally met. *"It is like an electrical current electrocuting me. It is like entering the people's bloodstream and their neurotransmitters. I live through the eyes, sweat and blood of many struggling souls and see glimpses of our universe, past and future."* From time to time she would explain her strange sensations with medical, scientific or philosophical words.

Although Akiane seemed to write out of obligation to God, like some reluctant messenger, she blossomed, reciting the poetry in front of millions of people, as if a completely new person with another mission emerged on the stage and in front of the camera. She became unrecognizable. From the doubts: "*. . . Okay, Okay, let me write this down before I forget, and let's just get it over with.*" To passion: "*Wow, these words are changing me and the world around me. Please listen!*" From questioning: "*Who needs my poetry? Why does God want me to write?*" To prophetic convictions: "*I see myself in all continents sharing God's love and truth, and throngs gather around to hear more. I see thousands get healed. We have to pray continuously. We have to trust God. This is our only protection and hope.*"

Welcome to Akiane's world of inspiration . . .

The Publishers

Foreword

Encountering the poems of Akiane in *My Dream is Bigger than I: Memories of Tomorrow* is to encounter a poet whose work does not invite commentary on influence, tradition, and experimentation. Akiane's poetry exists without category, a realization which places her as a writer in the company of the best artists of any age; the truly original artist is a student of the universe, not a master of the moment.

Akiane's poems are lyrical, meditative, dream-like, narrative, and visionary: herein we encounter the transcendent mind of the poet which creates the poem, and we become present to the poet's fields of inspiration. The poems' subjects offer partial yet startlingly clear glimpses into Akiane's inner world which both generates and offers the language and symbols of her imagination, intellect, creativity, and spirituality. Akiane's poems do not labor under the weight of rhetorical convictions; rather, Akiane uses observation, association, metaphor, and paradox to quietly strip poetic language to its crystalline truths. In them she urges the human heart to consider the extraordinary multifariousness of nature, to enter solitude with a waiting heart, and to be more faithful in loving God than in judging one another.

Many of Akiane's poems are the tender meeting places of self and nature: the poems often surround with white space, by line and/or stanza break, a single image or artifact: "leaf," "apple," "wave," "lightning", "dew," "grass," and "feather." Often these poems close with a startling observation: a statement or question which, like a koan, places us before the mystery of the world which we enter as physical beings, our minds and souls encased in the human frame of flesh and blood. In these poems, through particulars, we can reach awareness of the universal. With our human eyes, we can see through the screens of rain, or blossoms, or tree branches to the Creator's love of His creation.

In the first and second lines of the following stanza from "The Eclipse of Darkness," the speaker is able to imagine the space and time of eternity and simultaneously be in a real garden. The garden, cultivated and bearing flowers which are both "perfect" in their creation and "fallen" because they exist in time, seem to symbolize both ideality and reality. The speaker appears to have known *both* gardens: the perfect garden, and the one we know as fallen inhabitants:

> For all eternity
> I will be in gardens
> with perfect flowers,
> remembering and missing
> fallen petals of a fallen world.
> (Akiane, age 10)

As the reader travels through Akiane's poems in this collection written between Akiane's seventh and eleventh years, we see the deepening of her awareness and concern for the conditions of human beings in society, as well as the conditions of the human heart and soul in relation to God. Many of her poems, including the haiku-like short poems which close the collection, point us directly to issues of social justice, poverty, and the inhumanity of war:

> Roots cannot smell
> the scent of blossoms.
> A soldier forgets his mother's face
> to build a fortress.
> ("A Soldier," Akiane, age 9)

In this stanza, the soldier must "forget" or distance himself from the loving memory of his mother, his first earthly protector and nurturer, in order to build the "fortress," the defense against an enemy. With its beautiful parallelism of the two living organisms, the root and the blossom, and the soldier and the mother, Akiane reminds us of the unnatural wrenching of war. The distance between the root and the blossom is a natural distance. The soldier who must engage in war must cut himself off from love, memory, and connectedness. His forgetting is a de-humanizing defense mechanism, a hardening of the heart. It is a living death.

These are poignant, acute observations of the human condition, but there is also a promise of attenuation and faithfulness which flows throughout these poems, even in the poems of pain and human frailty. Pain is the felt condition of separation from God, but human love in all its manifestations is the felt condition of closeness to God's all-powerful love. In the poem "Licking Your Wounds," the pitiable act of a creature licking its wounded self unites the "you" and "everyone" in the common unbroken act of bending down. The verb "bend" suggests bowing, which in turn invites the idea of praying, and finally, an act of communal healing. The "you" is not named in the poem . . . does "you" symbolize Christ, suffering crucifixion? A human being, bearing human history's burdens? A horse with reins held against its neck, wounded, and then attended to?

> When you bend down
> to lick your wounds,
> everyone on your back
> holding the reins
> bends down too.
> (Akiane, age 11)

It does not matter. This poem, as do many of the poems in this collection, turns our eyes and minds to the relationship between self and other. The poet tells us that the universality of pain is not greater than the heart's capacity for compassion.

All of the poems in *My Dream is Bigger than I: Memories of Tomorrow* are centered rather than left-justified. It does not take the reader long to understand why. Akiane's poems derive from a center which transcends Reason's shapes and Time's linearity. Our eyes focus on the poems as though they are circles without beginning or end. In the poem "The Promise," Akiane writes "water can be washed only with water." These poems train our eyes upon Akiane's visions of wholeness. Their words for "water," which include "tears," "blood," "rain," and "snowflake" are the provision she has to speak of God's creation, God's enduring connection to us, and the divine cleansing water of His perfect love:

> My footsteps will always show you where I am
> each time I enlarge your eyes
> with a blooming view
> and each time I plant the paradise
> for you.
> (from "Planting the Paradise," Akiane, age 7)

Laurie Lamon, Ph.D.
Professor of English, Whitworth College
An author of *The Fork Without Hunger*

"... A reader is invited to figure out who "I" and "YOU" are in each story..."

Relationships

Soul is like a monarch without a crown in an endless palace of Relationships

Where each mature Relationship is patience

And each immature Relationship is a performance

Akiane Kramarik

*"The truth is still the truth—
even if it stutters."*

Akiane

Part I
Age 7

The Calluses

In my own strength
I look for my love—
but my first kiss gets snatched
by the first jealous dove.

I cannot feel my steps
when my courage limps—
I cannot see a rainbow shadow
in my glimpse.

With clay chains I cover my scalded face.
I shut my ears not to hear my God.
The callused fingers need to hold winter—
Next to the fountain the tulips rot.

The village streets are full of nails.
Wet mares still linger in orchard rain.
I see so clearly through my fall—
Bent pines will always hide their pain.

The Bells

I slipped on the mirror
Full of faces
I thought not of the future
Or the places

Hearts of pleasure
Filled with dances
The noise again
Controlled the answers

The words were gone
To change the smells
You dropped into my life
The bells

The blind spoke to mutes
The mute beheld the blind
Under heavenly bridge
Gushed streams of pride

The Sprouting Grass

Grazing cacti
in the desert
a hungry horse
I see
No one sees
the sprouting grass
below the sand
by me

Colorless dust
covers lonely stallion
I kneel
to touch his mane
Singer of light whispers
to my friend
as we fall asleep
in rain

The Divorce Of Resurrection

Your favorite fruit—
with worms.
Frostbitten eyes
cannot open or close.
Frostbitten eyes
cannot see what is in front
but only what is behind.

You turn around—
it is no one
but you
throwing a ring
into the flooded waterfall
for the divorce
of resurrection.

A Loaf Of Bread

Straining the peace
I restrained my universe—
Waves come tomorrow
leaving lilies
between your rivers

You saved just a crumb—
For me—it is a loaf
I am turning
like wind
towards your love

Clay

Cocoons got hardened in the weathered clay.
My day is bound. I cannot talk.
The time I breathe, the time I race.
Tonight the wind begins to walk.

Far away, no one sees my eyes.
I sing to paper butterflies to stay alive.
Far away, I hear someone love.
I will not leave until my time.

Like naked pine trees fall in ocean roots,
I fall without my shadow in the smell of rain.
Like newborn butterflies reach wooden flutes,
I reach your hand to be your clay.

So Much Of You

every time i want to catch a butterfly
i feel like a stray dog on a leash
yet dogs train me how to love

casting their thinking poles
crowds bang on my unlocked door
with cast iron pans

my bed is full of invitations—
inside my attic sand castle
Your hand is as long as my guess

so much of You
that on a scale of harmony
You outweigh the balance

All Too Fast

In the embrace
Of your youth I rest
But my childhood regrets
I must grow out of its nest

As your weather-beaten lips
Spreads our love and wonder
My straight back bends
To your blushing thunder

As if in one day
The aching years just pass
And as we hold our infant's future
We get wrinkled all too fast

Yes,
I Am Weak

Yes,
I am weak.
The moment
I turn one eye
from You,
I am one year behind
and I fall down on the earth.
My simple life
stands in front of You.
My great-grandchildren
are still your children.

Yes,
I am weak.
If I were not,
love would fade in my own reason
and I would not find Your wisdom,
where I know before I ask.
I used to hide
behind the trees You planted.
I cannot hide behind them anymore.
I can hide only inside of me
where You are.

I AM

i open a small shell
inside i find something small
like a pearl

and i hear the Spirit say—
each feather is a gift
from Me

the only reason the flight
between you and Me is straight
is because I let you and because you fly

answers poured from My thick truth
harden only questioning mouths
I waste the years of only the arrogant

inside the small shell
i find
I AM

A Dove

As I gaze through ashes
at my busy hands
at dusk I see a limping dove
with another bird on its back.

Welcoming weakness
the heavy eyes
of heaven
open the gates.

If love is the only true thing
we have left
how do we risk
carrying someone else?

If no man can hold
the Creator's hand
how does one dove
nest right in God's eye?

In Coals

Time greets me like a worker
and lets me exist.
As I float above atomic bombs
explosions look like mushroom galaxies.
Questions in ashes—
Borders dissolve like iceberg paralysis.
Who can sign a peace treaty
when races are in coals?
Which blessed nation
has eternal goals?

Scars

when broken love
searches for its own cast
worn scars
become indifferent
to touch

messengers' silence
has stoned the crowds

when dusty miles defeat
our limping gaze—
rusty trains pass
the indifferent graves
and we are left behind

light sadly invites
pretending hearts

someone's harvest
will be our hunger
but the change
is near—
for God wears our scars

My Garden

the flower pot
is empty
without flowers

and the asters
i am watering
will wither soon

so i will plant
my garden
on Your palms

where my shadow
has enough love
to see

and where Your shadow
has enough light
for growth

..S..h..a..t..t..e..r..e..d..

as fear
slowly polishes
melted candles
on time
a white clock shatters
on the wilted orchids

ripped clothes
are hanging
on a faded mirror
and broken chairs
remember
the deep moans

you sever wooden pages
off a calendar
and reach
for the copper door handle
to feel purple snowflakes
fall on your knees.

Between Shores

Leafless chestnuts are planted in mid-winter
To kiss my barren lips
No knowledge can change our past—
On my young eyelids melted candle drips

I sense the old age in my childhood
Where I cannot escape my name
I feel like a door—I wait for myself
My patience holds the sound of pain

Too many secrets lie on my feather pillow
My eyelids are too heavy to blink
The kneeling thoughts grow so many silhouettes
Night stalks me when I need to think

Next to me God reads the messages
My miniature fists are tired from a magnet pen
It is too lonely and too strange for me to see
Why I need to birth myself again and again

I think only once . . . to write forever—
So many triangles in oval eyes of wars
I name myself ocean
So tomorrow I could swim between shores

The Lantern

each night
the flies beat
against a lantern—
my time is late
and on the sunset
I lie down

my garden
is one blossom
full of memories—
I drag the cry
so I would remain
silent

white crows fly over my roof
and I see someone planting
my garden—
so beautifully . . .
that I want to walk
through my footsteps again

the wood chimes hold
the rushing wind
so the blossom of hope
is not blown away—
my time is late
but the flies fly away

The Birdfeeder

I count the stars with my brother
And guess how many sisters we shall have
One star pulsates in a foreign hue
The same tint as hope in our laugh

More than at any other time
We need to light the imagination cocoon
While sunset arrests the stars
A ladder extends from our bed to the moon

So the grapes will reflect our homeland
We weave a grapevine like a bridge
So stars will peck like birds
We hang a birdfeeder on the edge

To take the breath away
An irresistible color of joy arrives
Before sunrise evaporates the stars
This hour becomes the longest in our lives

The Knocks

Signing my own sight
I sign the dream
to dream

I knock
I knock
and I knock again
until a dent
appears on my knock

I knock
I knock
and I knock again
until the knock gets
stuck onto my dream

From exhaustion
from the delay of provision
dreams are born

Life

The first time
I looked at myself
was when I got burnt

The Spirit sent me
to wash
myself

So I could see her love
grow the future
of the beginning

Behind
an injury
is life

We begin
to heal
only when we hurt

We begin
to love
when sunsets are born

Is God's road
more narrow
than our footprints?

Today

Half built bridges sparkle
like ashes at night—
By themselves
the bridges do not stand.
I need to race
to hold the sign—
The bridge I climb on
shields my land.

I touch
your greasy hands
and with stitches
in my mouth I pray.
My short life
cannot pass you—
You need to live
a long life today.

The Nightingales

The first time
I smell the sunlight
there's nothing
but a fragrance
of cinnamon
Behind the last dusty drape—
dried Echinacea
on the windowsill

When no darkness
is in the way to drizzle
what shape
is the heart of a song
Though frightened nightingales never
sing in their nests
today they will—
today is forever

The Wrinkles

Childhood weeps
behind the fence.
I ask your old face
to salvage wrinkles for me,
so your age
could season my love,
and I could perceive your grief.

The branches
are not planted.
Wind chimes still ring
on the dried up oak.
When the future becomes
the past,
together we grow old.

The Butterflies

I climb on top
of your tender breath
without a testing wire
Wind-pinched juniper eyes jump
tossing the wind
into the fire

I need the nighttime to read my eyes
The mouth cracking the candles
gets sealed
I need a candleholder
to hold my eyes
and light them with juniper needles

Butterflies fly into my eyes
so I can see the colors
The years pass by in just one day
and like a blind child
I hold on to their wings
to fly away

A Wedding

pearl chains fence the whole heart
and the favorite feather masks
are picked
for lava faces

touched
we forget
all the hurts

love is a bride
searching for a groom—
let each day of our life
be a wedding

How Much Is It Worth?

Gluing bowls
and sewing letters
I sink through shivering flames
of the clock
While hours tick
you speak to me
When captured nights are asleep—
I walk

If I may dwell
within
your timeless today
how much
is my chiseled body worth
as I savor
my first and last eternity
on earth

Planting The Paradise

I lean on you like your favorite tree
for I am your child
wounded in your memory pages
where echoes weep
from theft
and where so much paradise
you left

I will give away my signature of love
just once more to be caught in your arms
My footsteps will always show you where I am
each time I enlarge your eyes
with a blooming view
and each time I plant the paradise
for you

The Color Of A Smile

leather saddles
drop off all horses
plowing without farmers
under the hooves of stallions
herbs appear pallid
and each side of distance breaks apart

behind
the slow dance of manes
behind the shade of a tree
apples drop with amber cores
radiating the true color—
the color of a smile

The Lips Of Wars

Birds who cannot fly must hide.
Chains fall on the cemented hearts.
Bruised footsteps follow plaguing fires.
And gardeners no longer find their yards.

Centuries will never heal the wounds,
If wars keep coughing up the rage.
Under the tongue of sin iniquity hides.
Bloodshed is a net in the cage.

Childhood falls off a tangled swing.
Sons stand up and ravens take up the shores.
As days peel off their heavy shadows,
Buried chests cover lips of wars.

The Ark

There was only one thing left to do—to create.
The huge waves began sinking my first sketch of Christ
and lifting up something else that looked like an ark.
I entered. It was empty.
And the quiet petrified me.
All of a sudden I saw someone stand by the door,
and I felt the hole.
The door had no handle.
The ark was pitch-black inside and out.

The eyes approached, but said nothing.
Then I saw an old man.
Nothing was touching me.
Neither hands. Nor water. Nor even air.
Although the days were not marked,
the days gave themselves away.
I was being filled up with only words and numbers.
I was naming and counting.
Naming and counting the young souls.

After several days I was filled up.
Someone was plucking my miles out of the wide road.
Soon after,
I spotted a strange clock that showed me the wrong time.
Then I heard: My portrait has no details. I will help you.
My name is countless sentences. All the numbers are my age.
And I chose you to see the right color of the ark.
I have one more thing to say before I go.
Follow only one way.
Remember—you are not forgotten.

The Robe

Love was walking forever until one moment
when She was shown the stairs
so narrow so long and so deep
as heaven itself

In the middle of one stair
Love saw a never-ending faith pulsating in space
Never-ending for faith
is always last moment

Another stair was filled with life from all over the worlds
Next stair was filled with truth which angels interpreted
Then Love landed on the Age stair
Same age as Herself

With Her tongue resting
She saw rains of the Earth crying for Her
Just for a moment She did not realize
that She was wearing God's Robe

The Robe was so heavy
that it pulled Her right to Earth
where children were waiting
to swing

In An Unobstructed View

Immature life changed
like a measurement for ocean,
like a measurement for vision.
The generations kept on climbing
on mixed-up altars
to defend their spiritual dreams.
And my vocal excitement
was bold and bitter from prophecy.
A myriad of fields sank
into the center of the harvest,
the abyss and the nucleus of infinity
that could be seen everywhere but in space.
My yielding and weak mind panicked—
Translated emotions raced through me
and my paralyzed eyes were filled
with a surgery of innocence
that held a real spiritual organization
in an unobstructed view.
On the mosaic crystal lake
everyone was adorned
in either crimson or white.
I compared what I saw
to what I ignored seeing—
corruption was hidden
in thoughts of possession.
In order to find the mind of eternity
the forbidden fruit of Eden had to be resisted.
In a blink of an eye the view shut down,
and a course of different breaths
affected my mind.
Who was awed by these images
was given wisdom.

The Departure

yesterday you asked for eternity
yet today nobody woke up in your room
and nobody will hear your departure

nobody will come
if they cannot hear your revealed thoughts
between lips

you blow away a splinter from your arm—
no one except your left tear stays with you—
you drop the tear in an envelope and mail it

there are no shadows on your boring floor—
lips have surrendered
but eyes do not forget

in your mahogany chair
you keep on writing
until a ball is kicked onto the salt shaker

you cannot think—you cannot talk
now only I can
and only I pass you a staff

having thrown out your shoes
now you want
to walk

The Trap

As I swim and watch the mallard ducks,
to my distress
a wave current washes away my clothes,
and I cannot return home.
But after a few hours I notice my clothes
draped over a stranger's shoulder.
There I see my ripped socks
and my blouse pockets still full of pebbles.
I reach for the stranger's hand.
"Who are you?"
*"The path you wanted to pave
is already being paved."*
"Why will no one touch it?" I ask again.
"Do vines fall off the leaves?"
"Who signed all the leaves?"
*"Isn't the light my signature?
Isn't the dark the eraser?"*
Suddenly my heart is marked . . .
And neighbors call my name.
But I do not answer.
"Where are you going with this man?"
I do not answer.
"Where are your clothes?"
I do not answer.
"He is a thief," they accuse.
"Who are you?"
I ask the gentle face.
*"Do not worry what you can take from here.
Whoever walks in the world-lover's footsteps
will fall into the most expensive trap . . ."*

Venom

At a distance
a wasteland is louder
than a warning—
I touch venom.

I tie love with a leash,
so she does not run away,
but she crawls back
to lie at the very feet of venom.

Poisoned love cuts a leash
with her teeth
and escapes like a wave
after drowning a man.

Only the memory of love
stays with me,
ready to move
stronger than venom.

*"I listened to everyone's advice,
but found my solution on the cross."*

Akiane

Part II

Age 8

The Lighthouse

Irritated by broken lightning lines,
I was tending flocks by the sea
and twisting a slingshot,
when inextinguishable silence fell.

Tired of tidal wave temptations and threats
the lighthouse began sinking into quicksand
and for the last time was lighting the way
where I walked without You.

The Waiting

In the distance
the scenery watches me
and teaches me
how to wait.

One foot—barefoot.
The other—still in a cast.
The waiting landscapes
my heart.

Rain
will stop
when my planted sycamore
is grown.

The Strength

I teach
and they
run away

I listen
and they
come

My strength
is
my silence

The Fingerprints

our afflictions
rebel against
the law

our failures
rebel
against peace

yet we can find
our blackest burdens
only in white truth

as the future finds
our covered footprints
we find the present

divine fingerprints
always match
ours

Under A Cast

Between past and future
our salty love
is a pantomime of taste
Wingless birds
exchange today
for tomorrow
and shoe soles wear out
across the lands of haste

Our wombs have felt
a scratching fossil
A dense waltz hangs
across a mast
The East harbor watches
our stormy sight
How hollow our pains are
under a cast

As the kites get stuck
on a cross
the restless wings
do not catch the breeze
As the wind kicks the beehives
past the doors
the homeless birds
pass only rootless trees

Gratitude

Out of how many blessings
we receive—do we declare?

Out of how many light questions
we carry
do we ignore the heavy answers?

On an equal turn
it is us who delays
and limits our spontaneous journey

There is no life
without blessings

Invitation To Love

Swinging
on chicory branches
lies slap an invitation
to love
with salty good-byes
and open the only bark
with an engraved vow.

Now both of you are buried
next to each other—
but the only thing
that has never changed
and never been taken off
were your wedding bands
and your commitment.

Trespassed

numbers on my door
do not belong—

kestrels perched on trellis
listen to the rain
scratching the patio windows—
perhaps the scent
will leave the olives soon

you cross
your freckled legs
and peel off my signature
pushing away the life
trapped by pyramids

you have already
trespassed
a pair of my eyes
that saw you rise
the millionth time

yet silence for me
is simple enough to heal

Shot Swans

When waltzing storms
strip autumn blossoms,
our memories of young meadows
fade in the breeze . . .
Humbled forests thirsty
without waterfalls . . .
Do lonely rivers
flow by themselves to seas?

Life begins to choose
the divine freedom . . .
Before fragile sunsets
birch trees break . . .
While newly hatched doves
are waiting for their first morning,
shot swans freeze
in the famished lake . . .

The Grand Piano

By the stained glass window
the brick-colored grand piano
was innocently silent
ignoring my journey
between its design
and its destination.
It was too rough to touch
and too dominant to listen to.

The brick-colored grand piano was so high—
I could not reach the keys.
So I grabbed my mother's stiff bracelet
and reached the first ivory key.
That was the only key
that sounded perfect.
I tried to remember which key it was.
But I could not.

Then I tried to strike
each and every key,
yet all of them were too heavy for me.
Finally,
I pushed the wobbliest chair
to the brick-colored grand piano
where I learned to sit
and listen.

He Had To Hope

If there is no water,
the boat never sinks—
so I agreed to be unnoticed.
She was too young
to see me born.
She was too old
to see me leave.

I felt improper
because
I deserved her.
But with such big eyes
she still never saw
the daffodils
I picked for her.

I was just another stranger
letting go of her arm—
Yet I hoped
she would cry in my eyes.
Yet I hoped that
savoring thirst
the hunger would pass.

Unborn Child

For an unborn life
once in a while
we walk upside down

A wall built just yesterday
is already
crumbled down

A virgin heart
left on the path
makes a sign to live

Whenever
you touch dew—
remember the land

The Chosen Echo

if no one reaches me
i cannot see

as mirror breaks mirror
hollow end forgets reflection
and the sacrifice of growth
corners the times

turning away from the heat
kneeling is broken
and for years i watch my fingers grow
while sore hands are bound
to my feet—
and for years my spine is being bent
while the eyes cleave to me

You create the ages
to control this afternoon
and i feel like a shelter for visions
but i need to seal
the rough lives i undress—
around You
the moment is all my life

when my weakness finds
Your stretched-out hand
i reuse my intelligence
to delay the struggles

but can the chosen echo
reach its own end?

The Clearest Reality

Compared to You—
my creation has no realism.

I am writing and drawing on myself
hundreds of notes
so I could remember what I see,
for my mind sometimes uselessly disagrees.

Yet the longest memory,
the deepest joy, the farthest sight
and the clearest reality
that has ever lived was Yours!

A Present For My Father

As I share
my knitted bonnet
with my father
and finish unbraiding
the cage of childhood,
I hammer heliconia
into his forehead
naively hoping this to be
an exhibition
of a loving gift.

His fine hair
tickles the blossom pores
and I begin to feel,
I own his pain.
I fall asleep
in his wrinkled up flannel shirts.
When I wake up—
his clothes look pressed.
Wrapping myself in gift paper—
I am a present for my father.

Off The Rail

my journey begins
but the passing train
will not pick me up anytime soon—
as my ambitions bark
i crawl unnoticed to the railroad
to relive my life
which like a train rides towards love
with a one-way ticket

bent nettles on the ground—
each with a ribbon . . .
hiding behind me strangers prickle my burns—
i sharpen the hardship and i rub my soaked eyes—
oh the time has so many crossroads
for the future—
but is it going to be next year
as i know it

leaves just keep on bumping into me
until a train
like a permanently dissolved thought
runs off the rail
and as i drift off
with open eyes
infinity bares
my own conception

Tracked Down

Inside an icicle
a trapped blade of grass
calls for the sun
to ice fish it

As I spy on moving thoughts
I borrow secrets from other worlds
feeling the influence
of one soul to another
and the circle of impermanence
turns inside out

Cooling ashes fatigue my hands—
Dawn tracks down my spirit—
embraces me and pauses
so I could feel her longer

This Was The Time

the more familiar footprints
became to me
the more i tripped over them—
the more familiar ignorance became to me
the more I wanted to love

was it last night that I heard the harp
and I could not fall asleep—
was it the crippled hands
that played each song in one breath
as crickets climbed a symphony

in the likeness of listening
the slippery lips closed
in the likeness of the need
the fingers softened
the taut and rigid strings

there were too many anthems
on the strings
of an unfinished harp—
there were too many sun rays
that curled up

this was the time
to go to Your house
this was the time
to bow down
for You were the song

Clay Cradle

As an intertwined gem radiance
distills deep sleep in the clay cradle,
beneath tender cries
sinking into the sinkhole of childhood
horns chase the hornet nests,
and each race races
with its lips.

How thick, bouncy,
yet slippery this lip ground is!
If a prison survives trust
the snow balls of centuries' agony
cannot grow any more—
The pain simply may not enter
the future.

Letters

i was waiting and waiting
for my mother to sleep with me in my cradle
woven of her long hair

i was writing and writing
letters on her forehead with my sight
so i would always remember my dreams

my mother was waiting and waiting
until You crocheted my eyes
to hold the dawn

Your Candles Are Soft

As the nebulae spread my petitions
the arteries just take off,
and for months barefoot flames whisper—
Your . . . candles . . . are . . . soft . . .

While the temptations wait for me—
on every earlobe an ax hangs,
and around each hair—a fence.
Yet a hollow whirlwind cannot reach my pangs.

On a swing of swings I tickle the armpits of the air,
and the hairy bees tease my bare thighs.
Maybe I am a recluse and it is time I stop living
in front of the truth and behind the lies.

From The Fenced Lands

In resilient oceans
where there are no days
too old or too young
waves slam
against aching shores

Under a thunder sky
colored in a strange moonlight
guilt touches frozen bosoms

Passion watches
our diminishing attraction
and the grain
harvested
from fenced lands

I Love You

A two-spotted ladybug
snuggles between my knuckles
and is the reason
for painting the barn red
but the oat fields
start chasing me
for my blond hair

And I dash
into the nearby forest
padded with trees
moist from the storm
where a single ring
swings
on a mossy vine

On the tree bark
I love you is carved
Like a brick in a wheelbarrow
the hard trust is the shape
of the forest heart
Now it is time for me to carve
the confession.

One Wave

Lost in the ocean I am with you,
Ready for our boat to crash—
We both have sunk our oars.
Although our home
Is just a mile away,
We sail in circles.

When you hold me,
Your childhood map
Shows where to turn.
And I hold onto your wrinkles,
So I do not fall into the ocean—
One wave is a journey.

The Day I Was Born

The day I was born
I met
myself

The day I was born
I met
my young mother

The day I was born
I met
Christ sleeping in my cradle

Free Will

There is no room to breath
with so many guests—
yet the scratches
get softer
with every hurt.

On a skewer—unpeeled oranges.
On a loom—both linen and wool.
On my wrist—a bracelet of feathers.

As I finish
sewing flax
onto my quilted loon—
in the sheep-grazed meadow
affection of free will blushes.

The Last White Hair

If we blink just one eye at a time
how many mirrors
do we need to see ourselves?

When the nights feel no winter—
the streets are winter,
and unfulfilled distance cannot see us.
In the last city covered with fences
we come out under the waves
to hear icy whispers hang across the aspens.

Every falling light
feels the pulse of wombs lost in dark.
Every ladder wobbles on the eggshells.
Every joy—crushed like coal between canyons.
The reflection of bridges loses its true shape,
and we get lost without a mark.

If the last white hair outlasts the pain—
the scars will treat themselves
like open wounds.

The Paper Boat

with its hung icicles on the prow
and a spotted muzzle
a blizzard walks through a seashore
numbing everything in sight—
too many emerald hail footsteps in the air
and a paper boat drifts away
without an anchor

the shore is never too small for a harbor
and the harbor is never too small for a boat

errors of silhouettes grow up—
against the cheekbones
the hair beats
like a storm-torn sail
and at the memory feast
mouthfuls of life
are gulped down

hunger toils for thirst
thirst toils for hunger

you jump out of your charcoal eyes
straight into the wrong place
and you slap yourself
to balance again on pain
I look at both of your eyes
so you would let love go—
otherwise—there is no history

any mind does not fit wisdom
but wisdom fits any mind

The Cloak

i still remember two cloaks
seamlessly sewn together
and hung on the bale

hearing nothing but myself
somehow I wanted to stand
apart from myself
and thoughts spun like wheels

the cloaks were too big for me
so i hung them
above the well
for whoever needed them

as i slept
my eyelids grew thicker
and i saw beside me
Christ in a cloak waiting for me

bubbling home
i was
a stream

The Last Lullaby

before the light ties up the dark
the time is born
inside the womb of heaven

the mountain cannot hold
the weight of the cross
full of humanity's wrinkles

the shut silence
turns over
the love of the last lullaby

an hour of demise
knocks from above
sealing the journey of sacrifice

as the desert carries away
the ripened scent of the sins
Jesus hangs on his own planted tree

The Relief

I miss the sound
of shallow puddles.

I do not miss any senses.
The senses just rub on me.

And I burn the light
inside my eyes
until only salt is left.

When the world does not come out,
a child rubs my eyes,
so I would not miss my life again.

The childhood relieves me
from the irritations of fear.

I need a hill to be my yard.
I need the smell it carries.

The Shapelessness

Sometimes snow itself
awakens the roots.

Whenever griffons curl down
like locks
the velvet paintings are kept
in a vineyard
where scented circles twist
inside the velvety cheeks
of a saffron
smooth like antelope fir.

Yet what is the shape
of the fragile saffron—
in my eyes
I cannot see?
When sight gets displaced
the shape of shapelessness
is me.
I do not own myself.

Outside the window
mature apple trees swing
and right on my toes
caramel apples fall.
Soles of choices split open
and from the high precipice
the sound of licking
hangs down.

Next to a graceful antelope
I stand deformed.

I Need Only You

I am old enough to stay a child—
but my steps cannot stretch
inside a tight skirt.
I feel like the time
whenever I press my hunger on a leaf
and take shallow breaths in the dirt.

My angels cannot take
the breath for me—
Around their armor—feather yoke.
My angels cannot smell the weeds for me.
They taught me
how to plant the oak.

Where's refuge between us
who can cure me unbroken?
Let me hold Your hands of dew.
The chimes do not slip into my echo.
My neck is full of leaves—
I need only You.

The Old Age

Like a pilgrim, a laugh visits
to watch the last of my face.
Glowing in summer spices
my eyes are the color of embrace.

Windows weaken from frosted handprints.
On an oak chest the will is engraved.
When grandchildren slide off each wrinkle,
the hands again become youthfully brave.

Arms folded, I overlook a path through a puddle.
I still can taste the muddy roots.
Clothes with holes are thrown away.
A mutt wags his tail between the boots.

I am close enough to my knocking sparrows
whistling like cuckoo clocks under a worn-out coat.
I limp and carry nothing but a crumbled ceiling.
The rush of eclipse numbs a widowed throat.

I refuse to stop breathing,
and every day seems the same as I sculpt in straw.
I look for my own eyes in the mirror,
but find only You and Your Law.

The Stolen Painting

When intentions question me
I need to rake each gasp
like a strip of dried-up grass.
Thoughts keep running after me.
I catch the flames.
When I run past the fireplace,
it laughs.

I do not need to run like this all my life.
Filthy anise stops growing
in my cleaned-up eyes.
As I run through my inflamed window
I see autumn leaves covering summer.
My wings of wilderness
were left in paradise.

I need pollen to cover my eyelids
so I will not see who steals my painting
where I enlarge your whispering pupils.
As I wait for you
I swim in your tears.
Only your maroon tear ducts stop me
like the dew hills.

Wings Over Me

If I could hear anything through my rainbow
it is the wildflower echoes.
I wash my clean clothes, but creases stay hard,
and feathers land on my stubborn knuckles.

While I wait for the soaking creases to soften,
ducklings sense my thirst.
Whenever I see a nest woven of wildflowers
childhood stays here to be nursed.

Just as my feet hang on me and follow
I follow the wings and beaks.
Only at sunset farther birds swim away
the closer they lean onto my cheeks.

The Pilgrim

traveling within myself
i feel like a journey—
my thoughts on immortality
have enough of half turning

but what is half of enough

the lantern has hope for the candle
dripping wax knocks on the glass
polishing myself i chase myself
and timing myself i sprint along the brass

between the glass i remain myself

i need to sculpt myself out of crystallized honey
so i can be lost again somewhere deep in clay
stringing my rag dolls through a clothesline
i thread myself to be here today

as a pilgrim i keep awakening the last essence of me

The Waves

rivers spit into an ocean
with ivory waves

sometimes boring
sometimes hostile

i am alone and far from You
because i forgot You

but when i lose attention to myself
You find me

and it gets crowded
inside

i have to kneel
before i dive again

the sacks of myself
are villages

and right inside me
are the bound lives

i have leaked and burned
i have crawled and learned

at one time
all waves do not come

Weakness Below A Cast

without any eyes but with so many views
a leaf on the edge hangs confused

light night before a dark day
reveals soil full of roots of the prey

moon and sun with the same deflection
rusts a steel with an endless correction

and like a stuffed animal
hollow love is ground in the sand-mill

bonded to the cast of the cliff
the heart paints pale love to live

"*... Each sincere confession is an identity mission ...*"

Akiane

Part III

Age 9

Spiritual Knowledge

the collision of busy feet
ignore the screams of roots—
a broken rake unleashes leaves

the agony of understanding sorrow
is the ablution
of inhabited consciousness

spiritual knowledge is uncomfortable
for it teaches
to console the suffering

on each fingerprint—
a surgery
of microscopic messages

The Price Of Feeling

Unrecognized
in its own backyard,
each devoted emotion is exposed
to the whole world
and thrown upside down
into a bitter trial . . .

Only the void
escapes safely,
for it risks safely—
Paying the price of feeling
can be like lightning
in an open field . . .

Consciousness Of Giving

The earth crosses
chasing desires
in the calmness of infinitude.
A crown—
on each crown.

Jagged wounds are filled up with light
so to blind the nonsense
that comes free with a knowledge
of defiled affection and a fool-stool
trying to reach bliss faster.

What a waste of energy
to try understanding nonsense!
What a waste of time
counting the square footage of the mind
that weighs the molecules of oxygen.

Yet pure consciousness
given
to creation
is the consciousness
of selfless giving.

Heart-strings

When we bear offspring to pride,
it is hard to give it up—
so we keep collecting stars
for the last defeat . . .
Commands are shaped
like ourselves,
and street maps
match the lines on our feet.

With a kicked ball inside the eye
and a cast for our faces
we find ourselves crushed in the mirror—
White is the color we have never seen . . .
Will our heart-strings fit
a one-wave ocean
as we wear our eyes
without a seam?

When We Lift The Shell

Claws
have been sharpened

But when we lift the shell
in the divine nest
love waits
for us
to braid her
eyelashes

The darkness
prepares our eyes for light
The narrow road
is a path to see the way—
Peace is the password
for the sight

Only the divine instinct
can pull us towards paradise

A Soldier

The noise of war
fills up your wounds.
On the shot guitar
every other string is your hair.
As your image fills up
the silhouette-less soil
life braids its own truth
of prayer.

Sidewalks crack
from meaningless marathons.
Gray corners
will be your portraits.
Roots cannot smell
the scent of blossoms.
A soldier forgets his mother's face
to build a fortress.

All Color Eyes

a hawk
with the shortest feathers
leaves the shore

and each tickle of a grotesque mirage
runs over the sumac
scratching the sketch

looking at my rough draft of the bird
i wish i knew
how to paint myself

amidst the gravel where the notes
hopelessly compare themselves to paints
there is live music and art

after leaving handless clocks
nights come back
to shape my serenity

and rolling between the sights
my confessions are stunted
by a falling branch

new leaves of the year soak until i am there
until i am at the horizon
pointing to all the colors in Your eyes

What Color Am I?

Pollen—
in the fur of coyotes.
The rivers judge the thirst
and a forest grows.
The first thunder echoes
to the end—
Together with other minds
I am a bare tree
and restless I learn
how to bend.

Behind barkless trunks
the tired waves beat against my feet
in an attempt to dry up—
and life seems slow indeed.
If no shadow or light falls on me,
what color am I ?
The roots are still attached
to the trunk,
but fallen feathers of a raven
do not fly.

During A Race

During a race for each race
chill blooms the air
and each pulse
throbs faster

During a race for each race
everyone looks at you
but still
passes you by

During a race for each race
an hourglass spills out the sand
and beakless running
mocks even the vultures

Florescent Lives

When I am young, I never see myself.
When I am old, I always see myself young.
And inside the memory of canvas
weaved into a rope
a single hair brushstroke like an overslept answer
keeps visiting florescent lives.

Gouache eyes drip and see nothing,
yet they magnify
the life of an oil painting,
where colors peck on each other
to find out what is new.

In a single hue
the whole field smells
like my brush,
and the frames in my soul
pick out the most extraordinary blossoms!

Only leather eyes visualize
how I pick bent carnations
for the inspection of my thoughts.
Between the divided tranquility fibers—
the poppy islands of my roller-coaster mind.

Tranquility always confesses
before entering the mood of mortal expression,
because it always fails—
the unknown crashing down
on the unknown.

On a warm windowsill
an old harmonica with sealed cracks
looks like a beach bridge.
In sunlight my breath is just the same—too hot.
Now only the heart can take it.
Maybe it has already burned up.

I Lean Against Love

It seems to me
that each time dandelions
are braided into a wreath
their heartbeats show up

The soul invitation
and universe freedom are free
if I respond
to their mute command

When I trip
over the past
and dive into a future ocean
I lean against love

Why then
am I standing here
blowing each dandelion puff
away from me?

In The Soil

the transcended dance dreams
of never waking up—
life icicles hang like wind-chimes

each chord-less embrace of the air battles nothing
just reaches the uncovered self
coating the eyes of daily composure

as you plant each self in soil
the sound of aroma waves so many welcomes—
rolling in shoots returns you to yourself

atop a weed . . . tied up dust is the sense
left to shrivel up and dive into me—
clothed in mud i breathe in you

as i move and wash in you
i receive each sweep
of recognized struggle

and swollen cleansing
empties thirsty mind
falling through slush of nurtured gracefulness

tasting the touches
and dreaming in each other's minds
i forget the unsolved substance of being without you

climbing off lightning
is our memory of waiting
that never waits

Next Breeze Is Free

As similar hearts
wear similar petals of love
our external days are within us

Immaculate eyes
are the vivid reflection
of a nearby mind touch
that instantly recognizes a lover's wild face
in the wings of a firefly
reflecting off the nightingale's eyes

Next breeze is free
for love
to create us

Eternity Thumbnail

The dawn pulse
is the oxygen of love.
As thunder distorts a crow's shrieks
I find the depth of heaven
in the impenetrable ridges
of an acorn . . .
Fields get washed,
soil lifts up the dew,
and lightning like a spiral of doubt
slides down.

I still pity myself
as I leap over crowds.
On a jarring
and steep peak
the limit for my footsteps
is reached.

In a rush
looking within the storm
I crash into the sky and mingle
with the creation of the universes
where I view
the panoramic birth
of a human child
with a crown of seeds—
a glimpse of an eternity thumbnail
yet an everlasting event.

Staining The Rust

Gazing through dew inside glass—
the future . . .
No stones to hide under—
the past . . .
Shoreless shore—
the memory . . .
Under an emotional microscope—
the stillness is fast . . .

Near each gasping grasp—
the air . . .
Stuck back to back—
friendships dawn . . .
Grinding bark—
the stumps . . .
Behind every horizon—
there is another one . . .

Dried Tears Never Reach A Rainbow

I wish I could view my memory
But the memory forgets yesterday's truth—
If love had enough light
She would never stay blind—
And with just one life left to love
I split the cast of my youth.

Lately every day appears scarlet to me
In all the hurts of a stormy wind.
Every time I open my life too fast,
It sweats—
And with each flipped page
I am asked to dive in.

Where I dive in—
It is autumn falling into winter
All curled up and drenched
Like a leaf of doubt.
And only winter itself
Can flatten it out.

Maybe it will take me
My whole life
To walk through all the seasons
Of the tide.
As my mind races my memory—
The memory erases the mind.

Too Far Away

The early roots
of a muddy shallow swamp
grow
into blooming branches.

As I look at the reflection in the water
that hypnotizes my trust,
handfuls of water
gush through my mind.

Embraced silence unfolds a sleepy birth
tasting ocean millions of times.
In wind-tangled clothes
I plant an acre of land.

Leading myself I am not aware
that the homeland swing
of matchless wheat
is not mine.

A prairie dove claims me to fly
and my own voice
tries to search me,
but I am too far away.

Thunderstorms

as evergreen minutes
float away
with white clouds

hail
falls underwater
disguised as a willow

cooled by dawn thunderstorms
devotion shrivels
and fear runs to the edge of each leak

and as reflections
of a planted jasmine
burst together with an over-inflated balloon

the wet clay face of love
tries catching fingerprints
from blind children

lightning still teaches lightning
to heal hollow eyes
for sight is motion

A Mystery

evil force is a mystery
rubbing the spears for your faith

you promise to leave doubt
but the drums reach eardrums
and a bouquet of thorns sinks
into your wounded womb

you slay your fingers
to permanently conceal affection
but leaving love
is not a victory

the future is a mystery
indiscernible to your carnal eyes

Too Blurry

With the owl's last call
of night
morning hums
releasing breeze.
But birds do not stop playing
with the moon.
On nearby pasture
thirst climbs on dew . . .

It is too blurry
to cut the blade of grass.

The whistles unwind
and branches get all entwined
making it hard to tell
to which tree
each belongs
and which nest
is pushed off
to predators . . .

White Kisses

There are plenty of guesses
from shallow to deep
in the young ocean.
Each time I move,
something inside does not belong to life.
My eyes water from saltwater.

Six fins come to the surface
and appear like a bridge
of continental lives.
But the loyalty of dolphins
is still
to the ocean.

I remove an oxygen mask
and only then each dive unfolds a sonar sound.
And only then I am brought to shore,
where bubble eyes stare at me
for the longest time,
and my flippers get stamped with white kisses.

Never Hitting The Ground

While the secured yesterday waits
for an unsecured tomorrow—
dust falls
into the cracks of a clock
slowing down a pendulum—
Who gulps down time—
wants to rest . . .

By the refused window
oatmeal smell
gets squeezed out of the kernels—
You think it is too late
to launch love
behind the piles
of junk traffic . . .

As fancy garments
get drenched in ragged downpour,
the prairie soaks your reminiscences—
And just like arctic falcons
without any feathers,
your eyes dim
without any hues . . .

Picking up the pieces
of lashed-up fate—
you roll up sleeves
one last time
and break
never hitting
the ground . . .

You Can Take Everything I Have

You can take everything I have—
but leave my love
As soon as December borrows the sun
hope is taken down and whipped
When I stand up from the sand—
the sand smells like me

You can take everything I have—
but leave my love—
I will not wait until I have
only one thing left to share—my farewell
where love is
on the other side of the fence

You can take everything I have—
but leave my love
Your shoelaces—untied
as in my childhood—so in your old age
At last robust waves request my feet
but a whirl-wind blows away my wooden legs

Adolescence

above marble
empty cocoons hang in icicles
formed from intense staring

in the morning cup of tea icicles wake up—
and eyes like butterflies
turn into arched rain—a rainbow

with or without
adult lessons
adolescence teaches itself

as man's promises
separate balance
marble chisels itself

Almost

I almost felt like burning
behind everyone controlled by me.
But I took only the breath I could reach.
There were too many days
in each face.

It is time we meet again
on a stage of love
that plays over and over.

I almost wanted everyone,
but I did not have you.
Now the life set is shaking my hand
to let go of the past.
Part one is falling.

It Is Your Eyes I Am Looking For

Days blink
turning dawns into dusks—
Kindling the eclipses
fills a single eye with so many views!
It is Your eyes I am looking for!
It is Your eyes I am looking for!

The saddles get broken from trying to find
a Creator to make a perfect world—
There is at least one bumpy road
in every smooth universe.
It is Your eyes I am looking for!
It is Your eyes I am looking for!

Gaining wisdom through the heart,
reason is born trusting.
Oh, the way truth observes love—
always in the corner!
It is Your eyes I am looking for!
It is Your eyes I am looking for!

Barefoot

there is too much
of plastic rain
behind a fence of vows

probing deception
the mind glares
and hesitates to walk in light

memory dumps
your absent presence
over the shoulders of lust

and keeping winds away
the cattails blow
on mirrored windmills

like a broken root in a river of infidelity
barefoot you catch each air
believing you cannot breathe

but it takes eternity
to know—
you can

Homeward Trapped

Roaming
through arid wilds
I hear a piccolo

Stung
by rivalry confusion
I blow it away

Yet even stronger it clings to me
with a majesty
of its exhaled aroma

How quickly I am conquered
by this tender
and hollow twig

South of my eyes
heart waves begin
to pound

Homeward trapped
I surrender
to be a faint lightning

Dizzy

leaves somehow fall faster each autumn
and changes just turn dizzy
from changing

challenged voices
get raspy
and abstract colors
harvest the moths' silk
which like trust
feels thicker each night
and thinner each day

what a low nature of mortality—
no motion—but only dizzy emotion
at separating apples of life

i try to fish out clover
from the quicksand
for binding my hair
looking like yarn
but i feel something
just keeps on blocking
the move—

crispy dew smells
fainted grass
under my feet

Thirst Follows Even Ice

Thirst follows even ice—
The mortal birth of immortal eternity
is love at first sight.
On the eve of our birth
we are inside the womb of lullaby—
And no one can choose for us
the time to be born or to love

Thirst follows even ice—
Spikes defeat cobwebs
and drafts warp
rainbow arches—
The indifference of our mistakes
makes us different—
We are handmade

Thirst follows even ice—
While nature is betrothed
to the fallen spirit
extreme weather still owns us—
but one snowstorm
cannot stand
for the whole winter

Thirst follows even ice—
Dipping the months into years
leaves finish their flight
on the ground—
Yet only underneath
mud puddles
does the journey of a leaf begin

Whose Imagination?

As love makes love
through so many lovers,
kissed knees shake off the snow,
and the kiss keeps its own taste.

Like charmed seeds
in the chains of chaffs
we fall on false faults in fading faith.
Our downfalls lose the exalted losses.

The kings atop their crowns.
Judging ourselves we become our own kingdom.
Searching for our own knowledge and laws
leads us only to poisoned feasts.

How many ribbons can hang on pride?
Pearls please only blank pleasure.
Yet not a single human
can create a soul.

Fallen feathers need to belong.
Forgiven for their forming wisdom
the harmless inherit secrets in trust.
Muzzles are sewn only for messengers.

Can we think of ascension
without wearing a callous?
Is God's breath—
a blistered oasis of His imagination?

Each generation arrives with its own opinion
about its own heaven—
facing the true heaven.
But worship accepts any framing.

The Seeking

each time
i stop singing—
in the corner of the storm
a wolf howls—
where a divine choir
invites supreme growth—
from mud
to flowers

uncovered gates
with moonlight stripes—
each shape
with a meaning—
as rhythm rhymes
itself—
the seekers seek
the seeking

By Faith

Turning away from the sun
sage still grows by the lava—
It is too early for stars to yawn.
Shoulders lean against my shoulders
that lean against Your gates—
silence hears nothing at dawn.

I need to outlast summer—
every season my wisdom changes
like red spots on a trout.
I increase my devotion,
but Your hills still stay alone
within my doubt.

When I plant finest diamonds,
my tears turn navy blue,
yet my eyes remain clear—
At the garden full of strollers
I give away my choices
in a wheelbarrow.

The shape of ballads
tastes like childbirth
in the desiccated sage.
An amethyst obelisk
misses dusty birds—
while I hide in some hazy cage.

Which eye to keep open?
The paper looks clean,
yet glasses today seem so dirty.
When I approach Your light, my eyes blink.
When I reach it—
they open for eternity.

My breath is nailed on the cross,
and for decades it smells like a steel hammer
following Your pain-free face.
At last, desert wind
blows away my footprints,
so I could follow You by faith.

The Ice Skater

Burdens carry on
skipping or tossing us
skipping or tossing us

Children come along
with their skating-rink shovels
skating-rink shovels

I keep covering your lavender eyes
with my stainless steel blades
stainless steel blades

But I keep falling and falling
just to make another hole in the ice
another hole in the ice

New Generation

As a snake rinses its head in mud
the past wars dictate
to all the enemies
who seek nothing
but annihilation.

Instant life
does not require
any commitment.
Terrorism, fires, earthquakes
and atomic bombs do not cease.

Ashes fall from above.
Cities, side by side,
completely burnt.
Oozing love swells up
without nature's scent.

The morning back flips.
Before night—
candles in the womb.
The closing battle of survival—
the virus of history rules.

The clay-cluttered door hardens
and confessions get crushed
before clinging to heavens.
Only New generation
is alive.

Only A Moment

Leaves crumble and fall
even when fully grown—
They are the mystery.

Next to a blade of a leaf
thorn daggers
soften like young cotton.

Under the feet—pollen.
Around the action—a fence.
Polished air—un-breathable.

Clouds twist the earth along with the sky—
The champion of strength
is a gray sparrow.

The dreams with white-coated eyes
no longer make sense.
But wrinkles last only a moment.

The Splinters

Sawhorses
and bicycles—
in the mud.

Inability to hide
had run over
my life.

Cluttered preaching
like a handcuffed beak
did not stop
until it understood nothing
and until all thoughts
except for those
it did not think of
turned in a spin-wheel.
Now
all the whites and blacks
question the gray.

The sawdust of ideas comes
from
the splinters.

The sawdust of faith comes
from pedaling
my first bicycle.

Not One Of Us

In giving—we find
In taking—we lose
Each breath the spirit made
now dictates to life
Your decision had no time for time itself
Instead of sharing the glory
You craved to own it all

Not one of us
has ever been created
with such brilliance
as You
Not one of us has ever overwhelmed
and destroyed so many souls
as You

Not one of us
has ever invented
such a ruined history
as You
Not one of us has ever desired
for the resurrection to be just a treasured lie
as You

The lies have a life sentence—
The truth has never ever
told the truth of the lies
Because there is no truth in lies
Because there is no truth
in You

Up Or Down

The urge
of approaching happiness . . .

You climbed up
full of questions.
But there was no more rope
to climb down.
Just the choice of
falling down—
to relive your life
over again
or climbing up—
to have one answer
for all questions.

But you chose
to stand against the beginning . . .

In The Captivity Of A Mask

the crumbs of invitations and a mirror
soak in a saucer

all the signs expect you
but you still resist them

intentions demand the time
from the energy

but you cannot understand the time
unless your eyes separate from obscurity

you reject the knocks
that didn't welcome you before

will it take now the whole army
to reach you

A Perfect Score

Each night
there is another wanting
there is another warning
in another dream
filled
with different destinies

Occupying tomorrow
like bittersweet cloves of love
demands our faith
but we have been hurt enough—
ready to jump off
all the combating continents

When both riches and rags
return to dust
and when both
champions and losers
are homeless
it is too late for obedience

As mortality separates
from immortality
everyone is stunned
to find out who is where
And only the love scars
keep a perfect score

"Do not teach others how to live your life."

Akiane

Part IV
Age 10

A Snowflake

the reflection
off a blind man's awareness
has sight

as soon as the snow angel is finished
a snowflake melts inside his
sleeve

he trips over the snow angel deep as a ravine
and counts each snowflake
falling into his empty eyes

the life of a snow angel
is never the same
shape

The Extraction Of Inspiration

Teasing a heart
digs out
a heart of art.

Through the door hinges
a child spies upon
the precision of life
forming
in the eyes of the portrait.

The brushes fight
like spears
splattering the paint.
The bristles fall apart
and land on my moist eyelashes.

I feel like a canvas on an easel
ready for a comprehensive anatomy
of the complete self
where all the strokes and textures
dry up on any surface.

I step into the paint for the last time
and adopt perfection
to complete the creation.

A Sign

Turmoil
overcomes indecision
with incomplete promises
and demands each plant
to grow
on a rugged path.
With all the crossed-over roads
and bridges
the trip continues
until an exit
of the highway
pulls me off
by a one-mile-long sign
Welcome
To Your Purpose

Endangered

Each oil drop
is grown
by watercolor eyes.

Watercolor
is a waterfront memory of neighbors
staring at each other at the harbor
like chimes at windows.

Providence
is wiped off a table
and your provincial faith
grows timid.

You are sold with your paints.
Now all feelings
are endangered.

By The Light

Against ocean waves
My senses hold eroded canyons
On a nine-mile-high cliff today I see You
From different scenes all in sync

Where inspiration is under construction
Where I keep afloat the universe
Where boat never sinks boat
Where tasting sweet air and fear of heights
Footsteps explore drop-offs

Only from dark coal tunnels
White diamonds come
But only by the Light
They are recognized

Hanging Upside Down

my soft clothing
were the nursing days
when blessings
were passed on to me

i had to fall
beneath the shade
beneath the dirt
beneath the light

blinded
by hard work
workers brought me
into their life

hanging
upside down
i understood
the ditch

This Is My Life

i came from beyond
learning to be
the breathing wonder

on the hanger the garland dress is alone
sharpening my hearing of tapping—
is there someone to hold my sprained leg

i hide from the audience
and replace the mirror
with a picture of the ballerina

with blistered feet i swing around
and turn into a swan—
i fly and dance—i fall and dance

i lift my leg above my shoulders and dance all night
until the breathless waves of a pirouette
roll over me

while the movement perfects love
the blush wears off
showing my clear cheeks

when my head is dizzy
when my ribbons are untied
and my tights are ripped—this is my life

The Perfection

Clay rested.
Rolling in it
was an unfamiliar nostalgia—
I lived in kisses, yet I could not kiss.

I pruned
an eternal proof
for a single perfection—
with an infant essence
I weighed eons
for an incomprehensible perfection
to compromise just for us.

With a pillow tucked in under a blanket
I woke up by myself
to inhale intoxicating chamomile
in a teacup.

The Sand Of Trying

Again and again traps are open
And thorns have risen
There is no rhythm
and no space—only panic
Between the slit quivers of a tight eclipse
the hurts leak out
releasing light beams from suffocation

Pipes are banged—
The sand is too deep for the nests
But barefoot races
will not stop drowning their tears
in the sand of trying
and children are dragged
through soot to be cleaned

The barren planets
are swept away—
Catching the fears
that wake them up
the dream wakes up the dream
the heart feels the heart
and the swing swings the swing

All The Crossroads

The rye field.
Sunset—without moonrise.
Birds without the eyes of instinct.

When the wind blows
my covert whisper
its smooth burrs
follow farmer's hands

Movement is paralyzed
and dry
like a rye grain
after a drought.

It feels I am too busy
and there is no time for anyone else.
Maybe this is the time
to get away from my crowded self.

When all the crossroads
are picked up—
the whole field is the manger.

Promises And Secrets

My imagined room—
My imagined room of faces
laughed all by itself
when it divided us.
The past cast my cast
over the necklace
of pictures.

The hardened life—
The hardened life now stares
at the alarm clock
waiting for the right instant
to awaken love on time.
Signs seem always tired
of showing themselves with secrets.

When I paint—
When I paint on mirrors
there are no reflections,
except for yours.
Under your inked eyelashes
in your blank eyes
I see myself.

While I watch you—
While I watch you now
through my binoculars,
your fur coat
is tied up to a diary.
Promises and secrets
hide away from their keepers.

Between The Wrinkles Of The Edge

Between the wrinkles of the edge
is the lost time—
an interlude.

The loneliness just like confusion—
a highway to yourself and a title of your life
is too lonely to grasp.
All the time crumbles down from good-byes.
Weak moths do not offend.
Your hand is full of them.
All toxic sight scatters
without any worry only for the blind.

The wind whips your memories
and pretends
as if it cannot hear the truth.
Dirty kisses fall off
the very un-erosive edge.
And metamorphosis of a betrayed love
keeps on walking on a copper maze
of dialogues.

For you each lava feeling
hardens and cracks like weathered pain.
Who can really hurt you
when all minds are gone?
In one of your pockets—
frozen blackberries.
One warm finger just like one prayer
has enough motion to melt them.

Between the wrinkles of the edge
you still have enough warmth left
to defrost yourself.

Brittle

i do not exist
in
and of myself

an aria from heaven
pours into my temples
and the melancholic wind
smells like
wild hay

i dissipate
in my own transforming shell
where i still feel brittle
just like shredded wheat
in a bowl

i do not exist
in
and of myself

A Double-Sided Sword

Ideal autumn twilights wild deception,
yet I do not own the lies that run away.
The eyes reveal more than words,
yet I do not own the sleeping infant's sight.

The flammable heart has closed
from the kisses of a venomous life.
Now looking at an umber brimstone,
I cannot feel,
I cannot touch,
and I cannot hold the pilgrim flame
meant to become cosmic fire
teaching clay.

I pity the harmless charges of the heart-sword
inside a thief's sheath.
The world is a double-sided sword I cannot walk on
where shameless eyes full of earthquakes
judge justice and rupture kingdoms.
The nectar dripping from a blade
passes by like a lifetime of listening
to an abandoned hollow mill.

The brick wall has a short life,
yet I do not own the fences behind it.
I am still a child,
yet I do not own the road to heaven.

A Bent Horizon

watching a bent horizon
i twist like a twig
i fall
like a feather
and the sky
looks empty
no azure no white no magenta
just sable black

escaping the domestic clock
and reversing
my circulation
i tumble down a hill
where alone
amid the glued mountains
i kneel
in the storm

with a stained blouse
i curl myself
like a cheap aluminum gate
to patch a busy ego
and wet clay
replaces
the futile claps
of my hands

Masquerade

in a year that is still ahead
yet has already passed
skin of the stars thickens
like an old tree
and short of breath
we sense cosmic thirst

welding sour silence
of the stoned paths
the fantasies swing
while the confessions
settle down
the feet of excuses

echo incarnations
of fake impressions
start posing for the heart
and eruptions of self-volcano
like an illusion
masquerade as the true light

The Eclipse Of Darkness

While birds fly over me,
the flax fields swivel,
and I become aware
of the source of growth
for innocently naked Eden.

The threads of my cloth
brush against the flax.
Eyes that cry out
desire no more
than a plant to be free
from becoming linen.
The orchard
is my responsibility.

For all eternity
I will be in gardens
with perfect flowers,
remembering and missing
fallen petals of a fallen world.

Existence

Thirst
is a rage of existence

The boundless urge
of creation
like an expectation
for thunder
in nature's veins
ignites desire
for contentment
with fire
at the end of its rope

For pottery to harden
flame is needed

When we kneel
we become the wise
and deep strength of love—
bigger
than all our wants
for all our wants are ill
and all our needs
are the consciously
unconscious love

Love
is the purpose of existence

The Released Arrow

seagulls in water—
winter explosions—
like windmills
they leap to catch the frogs

with my tattered garments
and soleless shoes
i roam
through crushed down bells

and drag the incarnation of thirst
to the restless mouth of a river—
where the salty
and fresh water shores meet

an eagle quietly soars
like a miracle between lighthouses—
immaculate feathers
still ignore the wings

i squint
like an invitation for war
and bow down
to the released arrow

Where Do I Turn?

The farthest person I feel
is the closest facing me—
The rock is finished I did not carve.
And the inheritance gazes at the inheritance—
The shelter itself may be the enemy.
In the cities of the mind—the iron chariots . . .

Refusing the strength of feathers
day stubbornly tickles night
with hard shells.
I switch caterpillars for the turning vines.
In the distance of malachite hills
I see their hazel eyes . . .

If I cannot touch your hair,
what do I see?
If my life is given to someone else,
where do I turn?
Like miles upon miles of smoldering thistles
in defense I burn . . .

Love breathes
through a snorkel,
and diamond polished fingernails
are layered with muddy flowers.
I need to hang on a mute swan—yet, it is a castle.
And I dye the light to remove the vows . . .

It Must Be Felt

like drained water
stepped-over love never feels safe—
let us stop dying
and start living . . .

what a useless chasing repentant attitude
if we never make enough failures to change—
if there is not enough width on the road
we will all be crushed by tomorrow

the secrets of immortality
lie within the simple dust—
its life is too short a road to be seen—
it must be felt

we do not need a reason to be happy
we do not need a calling to be happy—
let us stop those who ignore us
and listen to them

Across The Universe

You are too curious
to be perfect and grand for this world.
With trusting eyes
you expect second-chance love
across the table
across the street
across the city
across the ocean
across the universe

While an avalanche halts
inches away from you
the mind abyss
inspects infinity
in imagination
in hearing
in hope
in trust
in love

By living
on a road
that is too narrow
too wild
too high
too long
too inexplicable—
the paradise
never ends

Life Of Climbing

a waiting silence
between scorching whispers—
dreams are tossed

each step is a fantasy
and we return to our familiar maze

where spider webs
still collect dust

answers will never be answered
through explanation

but only
through a life of climbing

where there is no love
without pain

where scars and wheel-chairs
are heroes' reward

where wrinkles
are strength

and where grandchildren's
braided flowers into our gray hair
is love

The Hypothermic Love

childhood like millstone
is turning empty crowns
and the past weighs lighter
than today's thirst

in a shade—even in the sun
you give away your free soul
and inside your eyes
the earth cries quietly

only in anguish—the livid cello
does not like its own sound
and you scald your own fingerprints
not to know the destiny

in a sweating heart
hypothermic love is still chilly
and can get warm
only when it feels

Beyond The Exceptions

you are
like an ocean memory
reaching me
with one of your sneaker waves
and stinging me
with a shark's bite

stay with me
as i learn
that beyond the exceptions
destiny hears out
all the ambitions but one—
indifference

stay with me
as i learn
my lesson
that i might never finish—
only love makes
the exceptions

Forgiveness

while we are busy
looking
at ourselves
shooting stars fall

wearing enemy armor
hunger itself
strides
with a busy muzzle

as waterfalls fall
like grizzly-bear wars
canon balls rust
and swords bow down to arrows

yet even the strength
of forgiveness
does not ease
the loss

and here it is—our homeland
running through us
antlers first
like an injured gazelle

Life Of Frames And Circles

i feel blind—i feel mute—i feel deaf
i still don't know where i am
in this eclipse

each view has a walking tall meaning
but somehow
i do not rebuild myself

each step i return visits me again—
through horn sounds—
a lightening

remaining in this world
i remain just a glass frame
from where no hardened view is too hard to see

i feel drained—i feel soaked—i feel drowned
in this overwhelming life of circles and frames
where there is no burden my size

One Plant At A Time

When it starts drizzling
the grass gasps
and the mountain run-off
waters the vineyard plateau.
Although born together
soil for dirt is exchanged.

Trading our hearts for souls
is the same
as trading the young
for our own dreams
or comparing our own two eyes,
one eye to the other.

The album of a lake
is too shallow
for our feet.
As ripples flip amber pages
freckled love pierces
tangled up wings.

And chestnuts fall
right into the cage
bursting the bars
until the vineyard of scars
becomes frozen
one plant at a time.

With Dust

Commanding all of us
to be docile and shaped like love,
the voice gets peeled
to the core, like the earth,
and an unrushed foresight surfaces.

Aromatic laurels—
lost victory.
The weakness of an oak
is still stronger
than our own strength.

The octave between Earth
and Heaven seems to be always
outstretched—
For the taste of eternity
is meekness.

Pilgrims just pass by
without knowing
what the Earth could do.
They climb up with dust.
And they climb down with dust.

Portrait Of Chances

A portrait of chances—
I chase life
where a lemon color on a palette
has sour taste,
where fields grow old faster
without flowers,
and where fuchsia petals are
found only in quilts.

When I turn around—
no sculpture of me.
And just like a paper
run over
by spilled ink
black polka-dot pupils
run over
me.

Here I Am

Here I am—
in a barking solo exhibit
where my art is unframed,
and where I paint
the final details
on all finished paintings.

Here I am—
the most ordinary spirit
who thinks for itself.
Please,
do not chase me away
from my own sight.

Here I am—
rushed to sleep
as the dirt darts stab me
and my dreams start questioning me.
Yet only focusing on the horizon
I am able to disperse my trials.

Here I am
discovering wisdom
within
a billion-dimensional tranquility
where I paint your portrait
on a diamond.

An Aftertaste

A guaranteed life
with a heavy-duty plastic bag
over its head—
Breath dipped in misery
results in a bitter aftertaste—
Listen to a distance
and do not make an affliction—
a despair . . .

Only the despair
stitches up dust
and keeps mistakes large—
Only muddy shadows
cannot choose their pristine destiny,
for destiny is chosen
for them.
But you can . . .

The Infinity Of Beginning

The fog dew
is the reflection of my glance.
Tears are already
my second life . . .

Yet I still fear
to live a life
that has already lived
in the eyes of the future.

In defense chasing nature
is a victory of delusion—
Floating feathers of a hymn
are footsteps to the voice.

The choir on a dewy folded leaf—
I wither at once
and vanish
in the immortality of the finish line . . .

Confidential

Shallow individualism
tries to stretch its existence
with its open capillaries
by filling up
all mortal importance.

We cannot complete
and fulfill our life on our own.
The road to destiny
has a perfect resemblance
to our compassion and benevolence.

Those pursuing
a confidential road of growth
reach a destination
where there is nobody waiting for them
to share their mastery.

A Kiss

The chased wave
becomes my bait—
I shut my eyes with larks.

When I blow the larks away
an iceberg
gets carved.

Sitting on nails
that rip up the covered cross
I pause on a white stain.

When I turn around
the rain soaks through.
My last breath is a kiss.

I Am Yours

I found you in fear—
Please, do not deny I am yours . . .
Who can resurrect your stillborn?
In this short life
what is fair?
Bitterness of each interruption
will not obey.
Only the honest
still mourn.

I found you in fear—
Please, do not deny I am yours . . .
Whose mission is doubt
will bear movement
without action,
choices
without victory,
temptation
without conscience.

I found you in fear—
Please, do not deny I am yours . . .
When your brick life is interrupted
who is the first to be born?
And who will deliver
your own premature birth?
Light becomes an eternal sight
only within
the infinite dimensional love!

The Flame Of The Time

The scars are opened
to smell the wounds.
The stain—on wood.
The lumps—in light.

Limping through the fire of visions
it is too late to change the laws.
It is too soon to awaken destiny.
Grace slips by evolving into a crown.

Surprising rise of uncountable force
seeks angelic loyalty.
Quieting predators' fury is like passing
through a throbbing gangrene.

Unimaginable is the pain,
the flame of time.
Unexplainable is the healing.
Unanswerable is the judgment.

Last Beat

The confusing aromas—
All the fruits are fermented.
No kisses—
just tuxedoes and suits are accepted.

The end has already performed
time turned backwards.
Gravity pulls
the last beat of a drum.

All the gentlemen figure
out the truth
with a bullet
in their eyes.

Adam And Eve

we run
we run through all the fields
we have never dreamed of
but we have not learned
how to walk
but we have not learned
how to play

we look
we look through
all the space scopes
but we have not learned
how to talk
but we have not learned
how to see

we know
we know what no one
has ever known
but we have not been
born
but we have not yet
lived

On The Edge Of A Bridge

The strained cream turns
into a muddy vinegar.
On the edge of a bridge—
an engagement ring.

With a flower in one hand
and a bag of grain in another
do you choose love
or survival?

The impossible
never takes pity.

If you choose survival
can you promise
your unborn child
a life full of love?

If you choose love
can you promise
the generations
survival?

Not By Accident

In a race racing itself,
fevers
still howl at the owls.
There are no shadows
by the lighthouse.
Because today
there is no light there.

If you were there,
you would not notice Me,
for you cannot look at My eyes
and stay the same.
There are certain things
wisdom cannot share
with the world.

Mankind will not stop
until you stop
tempting yourself.
Otherwise,
you will destroy the whole world
not by accident,
but by greed!

In The Rain

In the rain
there are no shadows
and there are no children
with umbrellas.

In the rain
everyone has grown up
and forgotten
how to swing.

In the rain
white is understood
drenched
in gray.

In The Middle

Each haystack
is a shield

Tragedy filtered
armed yet unconscious
faith

Battles between day and night
flood the strength
bursting with a perfect view

Who compares
does not choose

The Race Track

The target—under pressure.
All fences grow old.
And time has no mercy.

The race track like a mill
performs a live grinding
just for you.

You live on the edge.
And you leave on the edge.
But simple joys are not for sale.

Confused

a torch cannot hide
from a candle—
as an elliptical echo
sheds
the altar of influence
gets altered

standing confused
with a brush
i wobble
each mockery
absorbed
in my scars

in the depths of me
on a loom
i weave a fabric
drenched with the unknown
and paint love
on the bridges

On The Cloud Stage

My cuts
are framed
and I carry time

I attend
the soulless rocks
you stand on

Without owning anyone
can you at least attend
someone with a soul

My decrees are ignored
yet wisdom stands
and waits

Until I fulfill the prophecy
by showing endless divine attributes
on the cloud stage

Pouring My spirit onto the humble
I will not look at the prepared knowledge
but only at Love

Panoramic View

precipitation from within—
the longer the road—
the shorter life
seems.

as long as it lives—
the tallest live sequoia branch
cannot reach the ground
where snails appear the fastest

only a panoramic view
transforms
third degree burns
into massive dreams

Celestial Warmth

Each moment in April love
is a stripe
melting snow cones.

For some reason
eyes do not blink
until the last stripe
is worn off.

Wiggling toes
in the fog
is celestial warmth.

Mother Loaf

bonded to eagles
in flight
i wear the awake touches
and touch others
only as much
as how much truth
i observe

each breadcrumb
smells me
as if i were
a mother loaf—
oh how much gentler
and slower we breathe
next to a newborn

The Tempo Of The Seasons

While summer was slowly digging
underground,
before it had a chance to mature,
it was eroded.

The grass was outgrowing
the stumps,
and a hurricane of leaves
became autumn.

As winter abrasively budged in,
there were not enough creeks
to fill up the spring oceans of the world
made from scratch.

Ports

a dent in a mirror—
a hearing came
and we have been deaf
since.

ports—
without instructors
vessels—
without a loading dock
for listening

all the cuts turn
color-blind
and everything
gets discarded

Atrophy

the last nervous trip
escapes
my mind

muscular life
is getting atrophied
with each adversity

yet chasing each fall
is my submission
to my own cast of self

where there is no one
to bother
and no one to miss

Prepared

Prepared to be frozen in winter,
prepared to get flooded in spring,
prepared to be burned in summer,
the wheat is a perfect place
for my engagement ring.

Each time wheat grows, it bends.
Each time it is old, it's a haystack.
Each time it dies,
it is loaves of bread
on my back.

Scabs Of Knowledge

We became
the equation of degrees.
But increasing man's knowledge
is the same
as diamond dirt.

Short-sighted obedience obeys sin—
Automatic heart knows only
automatic knowledge—
just like short roots
can grow only short sights.

Knowledge without substance
should not be rescued,
for it embraces
stage projecting egos
and the vows of the wants.

While nature is being watched
dull nails do not hold,
and bookshelves
like scabs of knowledge
fall right onto the scales.

"How competitive the truth is racing to an absolute finish line!"

Akiane

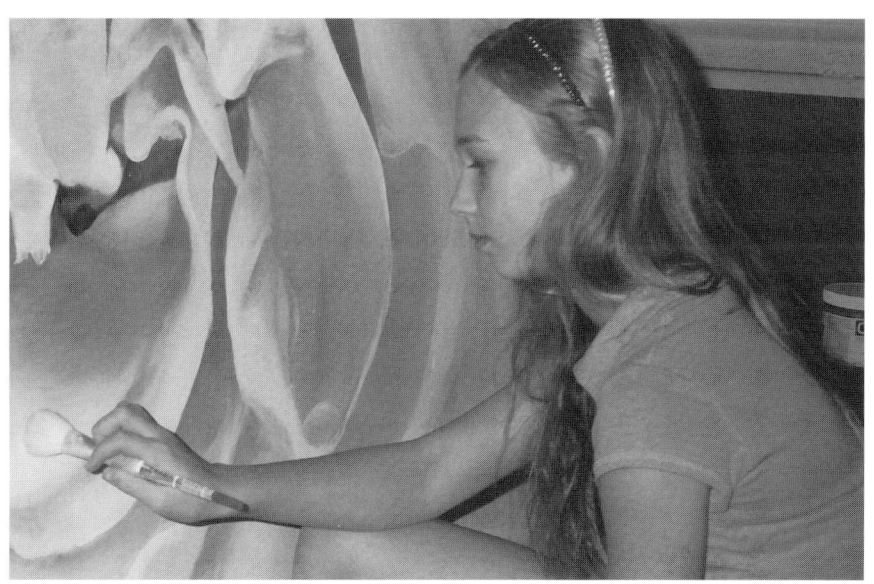

Part V
Age 11

Just One Of You

the frames I carry are too heavy—

the mass of senses
is not complete
without a saturation of cadmium red—
maximum control of drama and attraction

everything I view
has already been with you—
no excuses and no shapes of the moods
can separate us

impacted by light
and exposed to its radiation
my memory is full of you—
just one of you

artificial lights become subdued

Down A Mudslide

yesterday crashes down
a mudslide
yet tomorrow remains
unforgettable

at the dormant entrance
to the banquet
each tear like a jewel
above expensive rags
hangs on your neck
attracting madness

mellow silence—
in pillars
of exclamations
where elevations
and fevers
rise

one cannot win
contrast
by offering it
only light

Detached

each violin string gasps
as it plays
in staccato

spading gravel loads off each fight
destiny strides
with her dominant beauty

now separation
like the cramp of cheap aroma
is unable to smell love

sometimes it takes a cast on a leg
to understand the limitation
of each detached sense

Definition

Define the excuses
in freeze action
over a thousand-mile-long horizon

Define a face exposed to snow
turned towards me
at one degree

Define a temper concealing needs
The speed of light
will not catch its fall

Define the velocity of one lonely white
But do not define yourself—
Your direction will

Between My Shoulders

No one surrounds me—
but you

As I am standing
in sluggish air
your love
reflects me
and I find myself
inside
your caramel smell

One of my expressions
is missing
and my strength
is tickled and frescoed
Gazing
at your turquoise irises
my eyes get heavy

Between my shoulders—
my adolescent love

Invitation To The Scars

Infinite blueness—
supine.
All first-time travelers—
in paint.

Cosmic blemishes
anchored by size.
What is left is a hollow rod,
invitation to the scars.

I am born
wearing no royal gowns.
I am born in the corn field
to pick milkweeds.

Licking Your Wounds

You have lost all
who sat on your lap.
Ice seems deeper than water.
Yet it is not an experiment
of a perfect law.

The killer of each shortened life
is still alive.
But nothing can harm the survivors
tested on each equal point
of horizon.

When you bend down
to lick your wounds,
everyone on your back
holding the reins
bends down too.

Outside Themselves

The sap
from a broken maple
is tasteless—
Sunset rays
race a horizon
in each freezing raindrop

The first snow
without blizzard shadows
is too lonely to last—
and three hues of indigo
are frozen in the sky
like dried up palettes

Having given up their sight
wild eyes seek the true light
that does not spoil—
Only inside it
can they live outside themselves
where the wonder is never over

Don't Cross Life

On the farms
more food is grown
to feed liars
and false warriors—
Swarthy engine eyes
hang from an alarm.
The meaning competes
with the story.
Do not lie!
The blind cannot fake
sight.

I asked a thief
to steal the lies—
a masterpiece of deception
hangs on the walls of acceptance.
When each squeaky door opens
you handcuff yourself
and cut loose a frail prayer,
because deceit ages only from the light.
Do not cross life!
I have already walked
through it.

The Fence

I can explain everything
only
if there are no questions . . .

My acacia grows up.
With sharp branches
getting into my eyes
now I can cry along with wind
and forgive my fright.

No fence can hold a butterfly.
But under a chewed up swing—
a spayed dog . . .

In The Distance

In the distance
trains
like moving fresco walls
pass desolate ranches,
palaces and huts.

In the distance
a journey continues
until the miserable road
with a faded yellow line in the middle
ends by a cliff.

In the distance
feeble freedom begs for a reasonable mind,
and I recognize perfection
both in spoiled beauty
and rugged plainness of eternity.

In the distance
I yoke with mortality
while its winter acres
witness summer life
gouged like a seedless apple.

In the distance
through the soaked smells
I touch a close-up of faith
that starves self-exaltation
with pain-fertilized paralyzed life.

In the distance
an ocean is a deep thirst,
and waves like salted onion layers
get peeled one by one
making me more and more thirsty.

The Promise

Peace is making love—
there is no disturbance
in the steaming hot fruits
stretched in spice.

Different balance—
on different stairs.
Back to back—
a ceiling and a floor.

While sunset is observed
through a window,
the glass
stays ignored.

With tied up knots in a tongue
the only chance
that can be played now
is a promise.

A breath without a trace—
on top of moist fainting
just like on top
of mashed peaches.

Illusion has depth too—
the depth of despair.
A missing ring is a life of waiting.
Water can be washed only with water.

When You Leave

When you leave—
each breath cries itself
to sleep
and outside the dream
the kisses no longer offer comfort.
While vases break
they pause
to part from flowers.

When you leave—
every shadow
I move follows me
and as a blossom is pushed
into an urn of perfume
a branch of silence
is broken
from my tree.

Your Eyes Over Mine

Small and distant
I kneel like a servant
before a master
and all the compasses get shaken

I wake up full of scars from a prayer
and without any veils
at last I come
to celebrate certainty

The more I see you
the more I see
The more I see
the more I see you

The Eternal Terms

While clocks ignore eternity
tumbled by stones we tighten up zeros—
Impatient endurance is not growth

If we want to judge the world—
every thought and message
needs to be heard

Each light wave contains an unopened life
with a choice—
between today's reality or eternity

Let us not tamper with eternity
by ruining the only sample of life
given for our happiness

Eons of knowledge
remember our each breath
for the soul is the priceless treasure

We do not live for death
But neither does an eternity live just for us—
The eternal terms never waiver

Maybe the only reason
and the only way for us
to know God's mind is time

Among The Noble Hearts

I gather bitter flowers
just for myself,
for I have no prison—
Carry me . . . through the water,
so I can soak up all
I have sunk inside.

Thoughts like children
fight with sticks on both sides.
All I had is cut up . . . and now I am watched
like a broken crystal—
Do not shake me . . .
I am already shattered.

Licorice smeared lips—a delicious view.
You are dressed in canvas.
The masterpiece without my chains is yours,
reminding my unworthiness—
Leave me . . .
I do not have time to survive.

You could not take me,
so you steal my chains . . .
Today they are your city—
Release me . . .
I do not have the right to live
among the noble hearts.

I got acquainted with the last road,
and destination is blazing my eyes.
I perished twice,
but have not lived once.
Behind barbwires—
the scars of lies.

A Foursquare

Shadows
in a sunshade

All the apple-trees I plant
grow up

Each step I step on
climbs up

With a slip-knot
a hair-knot
and sand in my pockets
I skip on a foursquare

All the windows are open
and I hear flutes
either off key
or in melody

Floating leaves in puddles
are tired of being disturbed

We are all
a little tired

The ripe apples
are all with seeds

Inside Out

gravity does not rest
yet you still carry me
on your back

with the last tangled nerve
the ultimate spheres—
the eyes
like melted honeycombs
reach a dead end
and the womb is left homeless

my last moment is the memory of you
when finally my eyes turn inside out
and i catch infinity

A Double Life

constant light
is a constant
reminder
yet we trust
the double life

beneath a mask
carved on demand
an empty garden
welcomes
artificial plants

acting does not require
confessions
but where is the stage
if the whole world
is in wheelchairs

You Have Been Here Before

Punished by truth
love was grinding
our hearts

You lightened up our eyes
so the dirt would appear cleaner
to us

You spoke what was heard just by you
what was understood just by you
and was left just by you

It is hard for the mind to choose affliction
But it is even harder to leave the world
only with wise questions

Strength without a future
just like a kite without wind—
The soul deepens with each wrinkle

Men search for a goal in their own way
And you found the purpose
for everyone

An imagined light might seem too weak for us
but you have been here
before the creation

Cannot Keep Track

You cannot keep track
of what you know.
All the lies are rehearsed
that turn into soul crop-circles.

You cannot keep track
of what you ignore.
Anesthetics will not work
even on your cyan blue forget-me-nots.

You cannot keep track
of what you see.
Now you will grow up
with the world—
and not with me.

Before The Shutdown

Desert—in the water.
Dry smell—without any purity.
Mouths bark out of turn
at worn eyes
that turn the other way.
Each time differently.
Same answers—
to the same questions.

Leaves shaped like hearts—
with buckwheat arrows
underneath.
It is only a matter of time
before you shut down.

What matters now is
breathing,
praying
and staying alive.
Giving away
all you have
is much more
than keeping it.

A Pair Of Rainbows

The immortal tomorrow
blesses the mortal today
with a pair of rainbows—
suspended beauties

No excellence is given—
just work at the shifting borders
so we could taste hail
and clear the heartbeats

Influence does not conform
to the dull masks—
If we rest here—
we rest there

An Ambush

Above all the hours
of isolation,
above all the nights
without candles for calamities,
above all the aboves
you confessed
that you stood
against me.

Quietly you marked
with your venom
all the secrets of all centuries
that were not spoken
even in castles.
The lives that did not breathe
like you—
you took.

Once you had
the whole world,
but now
you do not own
your own heart.
You are planning an ambush,
but the whole world
is already empty.

A Battlefield In Stunned Eyes

Through the tacky clay
a dragonfly makes tracks that dry up
The gorges
are like rugged scars of the past

No one is able to smell so fresh
as the bored wild lavender
greeting an earthquake
on a cliff

Rich soil
of the furious river shore
is gravity in disguise—
where nothing rests

As fear fears itself
a fragile grip on the past weakens—
Structure like no other
solid eyes are impatient

You need to be noticed
so the moon elbow nudges you
If you are here—
you are already at the horizon

Prayers of vertical lives
grow without any soil, rainfall or sunshine
When you give your love to eternity—
it's a prayer-quake

The Missing Link

The night marble hills are crushed
the hopeless are left behind in luxury—
where obsessions drain life,
where enough
is never enough.

A simple brick makes the tower
from where all feelings
bear endless views—
The truth does not choose everyone,
and opposites never miss a fight.

The missing link
between personalities
is a perfect perspective—
a dimension outside reason
and a life of love flowing upstream.

But how long can we observe it
at a distance,
growing like pasque flowers in between
inside the dirt
that is older than we?

When belongings get attached to our emotions
we become an imaginative prison—
yet all the un-chased treasures
eventually find us,
so we could live a masterpiece of life.

The Divine Wrinkle

An ant is waiting
for a puddle to dry up
the whole day

All the rain
fits
one of my mittens

On the ground
right in front of a sodden wreath
holly-scented breeze stops

I breathe in
the first snowflake
and feel a divine wrinkle

The Lies

When sunsets appear in midday—
it is the mid-winter.
Onion winter sleeps in,
and we wake up with spring cries:
the feet are sore—
all the cuts have been stabbed twice.

For many it is nature
that catches us in a fighting lie,
wearing an armor of drowsy honeysuckles.
Many want to find answers
about the dark—
but few yearn for the light itself.

No one can pretend
to forgive truth,
except for the lies,
and only the lies can answer
all the questions
in this lifetime.

I Cannot

I cannot talk to fire—
It back-talks in flames

I cannot be in charge—
Just because I stand

I cannot catch all the shooting stars—
The dust still chooses me

I cannot hide in a prophetic silence—
No one will believe me

I cannot enter a palace in my rags—
Only love is royal

I cannot light up the whole world—
It is already burning

Mistakenly Mistaken

if there was not a divine palette
there would not be
anyone
anyplace
anytime
to balance an oak easel
on the hardwood floor

if there was not a brushstroke
crossing over the rules of vision—
an impressive gauge of accuracy
there would not be
an expressionistic painting—
a short cut
to the banquet of independence

if there was not a laugh
laughing at me
there would not be
an unveiled picture
that is not blank
but white—
my titanium kingdom

Profile Of Landscape

Wind swings in silence.
On the rolling sand dunes—
smooth sand castles.

Watching beige clouds
no comprehension
is needed.

Everything
seems to mature
to finishing touches.

Light adjusts
to a strange wedding
on the shoreline.

And the profile
of landscape
seems no longer effortless.

Without Me

Your hardy love is waiting for me
in the snow from all the sides
just like white snowflake prayers
in the sky wait for you.

Magnets get sawed.
I rush through the evening
without saying
good-bye.

The ballads linger on the swing sets
for anyone to sing them.
Do not be sad—
Today I am not praying for you.

So many futures
that tangle up the pasts,
but won't even comb
through the present.

Braid me,
so no-one would recognize me.
The chilly water looks
so transparent without me.

The Heart-Express

time is so fast
when it runs, it trips us—
small world tries to be on time
and changes like an impulse
or a disposable gift

all hardened from imitating gold
and unable to feel the surge
of even the most simple expressions
desperate heart-express hyperventilates
commandments of love

only a defenseless and humbled life
can appreciate patience of love
yet each sweat makes its own law—
greed ignites lies
and the lies ignite haste

the only ignored sound left
remains silence—
but living inside the avalanche
we always run—
but living fast is living a separation

A Fractured Game

our road misses gravel
where each pebble
contains all roads
and we all play a distance—
each time we thirst
we thirst
for more journey

but the horizons
seem too distant
to know
what we have endured
and mastered

the heart has always been
close to the edge
and many tried to push it off—
tide by tide
gust by gust
dust by dust
the edge is coming closer

The Memories Of Tomorrow

The world is a loud alarm.
Puddles of war
splash against a short silence.
I forget
where yesterday was.

Perhaps I have drowned
in the very pale lives
I failed to encourage.

Secret shelter
is offering me comfort,
but I am carried
to winter primroses,
the memories of tomorrow.

Return Our Hearing Eyes

In debt to anemic senses
huge signature of legend archives
is left behind.

Heavy castles cannot hear—
our orchard stopped growing
and we leave.

Barren blossoms
grew tired from closing
and opening false hope.

Instead of insects wearing the smell of blossoms,
now the pressure and volume of the scent
is on us.

And many of us simply long for joys
without the truth—
making life vulnerable to an invasion.

Dissecting beauty and peace
creates
counterfeit righteousness.

Return our hearing eyes,
so we could distract bandaged bombs
incapable of creating splendor.

War does not care
how beautiful
we are!

In The End

In the end
a living silence always turns
into communion . . .

A thunderstorm drenches
sun-dried fruit
and lays the hoods
on all heads.
Capricious icicles melt
inside the eyes
and wash away stones
within the refills of sanity mines.

Now darkness chases
to interrogate.
Hollow swords—its modern lie.
Nothing feels so numb
as an end of a dream.
Yet few are left
to see it.

Common sense nibbles
the unfathomable—
compassion lifts up
all the needs,
but the wants
are no longer content—
Shrewd beggars—
a cosmic decay.

In the end
all the laurels fall
on the ground . . .

All Of You

Time crinkles up as if it were you,
and trees bark
at all the mismatched leaves.
Above the highest
and the most prideful branch—
there is all of you.

Your transparent life
falls to the ground,
and the altars of the self shrivel—
A hail-squall
does not pamper the cells.

You cling to what will not last—
your life.
The entrance to the next world
is not wide enough
for both pride
and indifference.

Colorless—
you become any color.
If it does not matter
who you are
your enemies will show you
where you belong.

Supreme Sanctuary

Eternal childhood—
with delicate demands . . .
No reflections have been gathered
in the same-hue gardens—
A journey
seems too physical
across the crossroad of bridges.

Arriving at your dusty
but light palette
my hand touches
an opposite crossroad of a garden
overlooking
a single dimensional bench
by a gazebo.

There is a supreme sanctuary—so rare
that a falling luminosity is fluid
and can be captured.
All of its changes
are layers of immaculacy gardening life
where each fragrant flower
I put into my hair is a butterfly.

Permanent maps of curly wind
challenge all lanterns.
Only Light could show me where I am
by throwing ropes of colored aroma
to impatient foliage.
Inside the light of a blossom
the day never ends.

For some reason I cannot wait
to be mixed up
into the chaste pigments of all experiences.
For some reason
I cannot wait for the journey
which is the only way
to reach the Light.

Delicate Reflection

My door is hollow—
Patience is so busy being obedient—
but my heartbeat
is too loud.

In thirst
all the views are costly.
Soft texture of a long lasting mind—
the compassion is a delicate reflection.

There is no change
with upside down walls.
There is no stillness
with horizontally vertical doors.

All broken branches are tied up along with me—
I collapse floors with an upright confidence
and the unknown with a mind of its own
hears me out.

For those
who are placed upside down—
waterfalls do not fall—
but rise.

Not Yet

As you walk
as you pass
there is no romance
or balance in the voices
just a chilly laughter
Do not mix with the crowds yet—
The spirit has not
changed them

As you walk
as you pass
you defend all the defeated
and defenseless fears
but gold still refuses to be sifted
Do not blossom yet—
All the shovels are looking
for you

As you walk
as you pass
there is a helmet on each crown
and life seems like an illusion
that can never be conceived by you
Do not open your eyes yet—
The cages are still bigger
than the land

My Dream Is Bigger Than I

Romancing
white lighthouses
and dusting the nectar of air,
the seagulls freeze
my consciousness lead.
There is no flight beneath the wings—
the flight is ahead.

I ignore the skies cut up with clouds,
for dreams ignite
from the storms of the mind.
Daisies inside raindrops
fill up the winking eye of the childhood,
and I pull down
a child's hood.

The unborn dream of growth struggles.
The born struggle to dream.
But I refuse all choices
in exchange
for impossibility.
Only a dirt road
is without any speed limit.

Releasing a young bird
from a solid cliff
for the first time
even the smallest feather
learns how to fly.
And measuring myself I kiss my wishes.
But my dream is bigger than I.

Love

Love is never alone
Love is always crowded
Love is the shared self

We cannot own our love
And we cannot teach our love

The longest breath of love
is the shortest distance to heaven

The deepest life is love
The deepest love is an embrace

Love is not rest
Love is peace
Love is the purpose

> "*Rehearsing our own imagination
> we miss the recital of reality.*"
>
> Akiane

Part VI

*Reflections
Ages 7–11*

Connection

Without the mind
our hearts control
our speech.

Without the heart
our minds control
our hearing.

Beliefs

As we wait for rough beliefs
to be sharpened like spears
wood-peckers peck
on our oversized sheaths

Refused Defense

With its holy turban
trust is picked like a grain—
Embracing the counselor of justice
I inhabit
the fortress of refused defense

Childhood

Sometimes childhood
seems like a tender flower
with a slow and selfish sight
in an unfenced dense woodland

The Provider

i awake
with the snail-house
on my back
and a warbler feeder nailed
to my shell

The Glued Friendship

Before I glued
the rocking chair
my friend was rocking
there.

Inside My Shell

branches fell—
so many summers came and left
but i waited and waited
for summer inside my shell

Passing Sweetness

When admiring eyes savor the bliss
of the never lighted candle
every move of a slow dance
seems like eternity—
Passing sweetness
is the timeless last moment

A Contest

Trying to convince everyone
I have the widest smile
I frown

The Drought

As I feast—
the dawn clouds are stripped—
The drought

The Irony

Measuring circulating dust
we sweat in buildings
we have never built

Too Anxious

Too anxious
to seek harmony
we get discouraged

Depression

Depression is like glue.
The longer it touches you,
the harder it is to take it off.

Taxes

Tax collectors
pay taxes too

The Intruder

The intruder
does not like
the invitation

Entrapment

Preoccupied impression
is concerned only about the show—
Looking only at a peacock's feathers
entraps the heart.

Hope

When grass starts growing on the sun
and becomes the green light—
it is hope

Emptied

The first filled up wallet
was emptied
by the first choice

The Phenomenon

The phenomenon of the Spirit
cannot be measured—
Do we hold the frame
or does the frame hold us?

The Fight

When a soldier falls
into his own sheath
he fights against his own sword

Blocked Imagination

On a wall
I frame a nut in a frame of shells
and then I frame the frame with a lock.
A splitting headache finishes the rest . . .

Measuring

Measuring time energy is wasted
and the time changes

The Riddle

Between your eyes—your sight
The riddle is the only life
when words are needed

Gossip

By gossiping about truth
without living it
we cannot recognize perfection

Tranquility

Infirmity
Transcends
The senses
If
Tranquility
Is its
Transport

The Meaning of Life

The meaning of love
defines
the meaning of being born

The Rest

To see the rest
one can be lost
with the rest

The Surgery

The surgery
for the loneliness—
the altruism

Division

The
Transgressor's
Intervention
Is
Division

Breathing

The joy and agony of birth
is breathing

Competitive

How competitive the truth is
racing
to an absolute finish line!

Restrained

Unguarded honesty
gets restrained
by the strangers' defenses

Self-exaltation

Self exaltation exhausts
and reveals our lack of taste

Rules

It is easy to keep rules
we give to ourselves
not by someone else.
Ridiculing the stumbling rules of life
and pretending to be perfect
in our own realized dreams
we ridicule love

Still The Truth

The truth is still the truth—
even if it stutters

Infection

With an infected faith
not even the smallest component of the Supreme
can be known

Vanity

Vain and selfish curiosity
awakens the immorality
of eternal dissolution

Checkmate

Invading the universe altar
accusations checkmate
their own future

Flattery

To espouse flattery
is
escapism

Justice

Justice empowers.
But if the distance is established
the laws are discarded
and justice is smeared.

Jealousy

Jealousy knows
no remorse

Fame

fame
just like fur
sheds too

Sharing

We cannot own
our own sharing

Purity

The filth
has known purity.

But purity
has never known the filth.

Tragedies

Into the flood
of a soul
do not throw
even a pebble
for tragedies come
with the deepest memory currents

Permission

Humiliation and shame—
just like bungee jumping—
is my own invention
and permission of self-torture

Affection

The warmth of your affection
is the windshield wiper
in my eyes

Distraction

The view distracts
my interview with myself

Fired

Sunrise keeps the pressure
on each desert wildflower,
and the sun gets fired for a drought.

Lack Of Air

Sometimes it is the lack of air
that inhales the impulse
of transforming world history.

Gauge

The infancy in us
like a gauge of soul
measures our spirit

Doubt

The future or the past
never doubts—
only the present.

Perfection

I might be unable to be perfect
but I am able
to follow perfection

A Title

God's name
is not
a title

Offspring

Dignified freedom
is always the offspring
of the most attractive love

Fuel

the stop light for the ambitious
is fuel for the ride

Solution

I listened to
everyone's advice,
but found
my solution on the cross.

Unread

Reading other minds
does not mean
you read your own

Transgression

Transgression
of a lie detector
reveals whose
truth is next

The Distress

I distressed the cold-blooded heart
by putting it
on the mirror

Boredom

Boredom
wastes
time

Doubt

Sailing with a thirsty sight
doubt sees the shore
as just a drifting log in the ocean
and tries quenching our thirst
with salt water

Just Because

Just because you live
does not mean
you are alive

Life Extension

Human experiments
on a significant life extension
is a waste

Immature

Many mortals are too immature
for true visions
for they mix them up
with their own imaginations.

Foreknowledge

Foreknowledge
comes
with the crumpled up
instructions

Unfamiliar

knowing what you have tried—
your efforts might still be unfamiliar
with both time and humor

Those That Follow

those that follow men—
follow

those that follow love—
lead

Oblivious

believing all news
grown up wishes remain oblivious

Thrown Out

eyes cannot see themselves—
i cuddle silence
and i see my mother
for the last time

i envision myself full of hugs
running with a ball up and down the hills—
if i am reached from above
i will never let go

A Farmer

On a broken window—no dust.
On a front door—no mail box.

Next to the hogs in the hay
four hens lay warm eggs.

Even when I sleep
my fingers keep on planting.

Dumped

Accessories of selfishness—
dumped abilities in the dumpster

Mediocrity

Resistance of the challenges
is removed
for consumption of mediocrity

Rehearsal

Rehearsing our own imagination
we miss the recital of reality

For Life

Delicate creation—
with spiritual batteries
for life

A Ripple Effect

Only a meaningful conversation
produces a ripple effect
of eternal resonance

Gems

Gems are kept deep
and away from our sight
so we would dig

Effort

A promise demands our effort
An exhaustion defines our effort

Knowing The Unknown

Man
may love the impossible
God
can do the impossible

Knowing
the unknown
we convince our passion
of patience and hope

Missing

By missing my time
I wasted it more.

Dispositions

Some dispositions are like butterflies
that can endure
neither a passionate kiss
nor a corrective surgery

Help

Bold strength
always has bold help

Moved

It takes only a moment
to create and move a purpose.

But it takes sometimes a lifetime
to let the purpose move us.

Mission

Each sincere confession
is an identity mission

The Formula

Being see-through
dismisses the minds

Being clear
attracts the minds

Anger

Punching holes in walls
will not stop our anger
but will only stretch it further

The Spotlight

the spotlight identifies
both our appearance and endurance

Argument

an argument we participate in
reveals more about us
than any degrees or diplomas

Dry Waiting

Dirt was all over you
and your washed out clothes
hung dry for days

Who You Are

Being immature speaks of who you were.
Being mature speaks of who you are going to be.
Who you are is what you become.

The Virus

The virus of hatred and arrogance
will never have an opportunity
to receive justice

The Same

How awful—
Everyone looks
and acts the same!

Source

The lanterns wonder
where the light
at the end of a tunnel is

Teaching

Do not teach others
how to live your life

A Man's Love

There is not much there
to understand a man's wants

But there is too much
to understand a man's love

Building

keep on building rock castles—
until you know others

keep on building sand castles—
until you know yourself

A Chance

One needs
to have a chance
to give a chance

Load

Equal burdens
are convinced
that only their own load is heavier

Friendship

The un-compared knowledge
is friendship.

Injection

You need to be a mortal
with a muscular heart
to withstand the memory injection
of superficial entertainment

The Statue

One day
you walk
by a statue

The next
you become
the statue itself

Temptations

Most temptations arise
not because of ignorance
but because of ignoring the answers
that keep on flashing in front.
Only those who master faith
are able to control the temptations.

The Cleansing

Next to the house
hung clothes are drying

Oh how I feel like
washing myself now

The Persuasion

As the wind blows away my sandals
The lightning ignites my candles—
Today I am staying home

The Circle

the invitation
invites
itself

Cause And Effect

I misspell the question
I miss the answer

Disorganized Help

The excuses
act out my actions

The Influence

the audience changes
the diapason of the choir

A Legal Heart

You
kidnap
yourself

The Bridge

I correct the length of the river—
I saddle it

Overindulgence

permanent adventure
dulls excitement

Useless

The
Wasting
Is mad
That no one
Is using it

Envy

everyone
plays
your
meant
to be
life

The Theft

I rebelled
against someone
who did not

The Amnesia

I wish
I wished
I had a wish

The Measurements

The clock, the map, the scale,
the compass, the telescope, the thermometer,
the microscope,........................the prayer ...

The Joined Roots

So many questions
there are on this side of infinity
blending soft minds.
But true teachers learn from learners.

Patience

We never find patience by looking for it.
We find patience by looking for a purpose.

And the more we hurry for patience,
the longer it takes us to reach it.

The Silent Mask

The only time
you hear the crow sing
is when it is silent

The Bribe

You could at least
bribe your anger
so it would stop

Levitation

You have devoted your whole life
to learning how to levitate,
but you failed to notice
the needy on the ground.

The Contentment

My arms
have outgrown my coat

but for the first time
it keeps me warm

The Competition

Although the race has ended
the competitors still race

Emptiness

Emptiness never dies
because it has never lived

God never dies
because He has always lived

The Attachment

I am a half—
my injury
has left

Above The Daring Eyes

Wiping the whips the children think
the thoughts of others
making inspection of infinity dirty.
The shelter is above the daring eyes.

Except For Love

You can not talk, hear or reason.
And you can not know
that love is too heavy for you to carry,
but it is not too heavy to follow.
Soon you will be gone.
And perhaps no one will notice,
except for love herself.

The Prisoner

When the future
and the present meet each other
the air breathes without me
and the mail reaches my last home

Along with snow
falling on its own shadow
I will become
the very owner of my prison

The Sailor

I traveled many places
but I have not found one place like the earth
where faith can find any heart
on the very anchor of the ship.

The Cure

A diapason of disobedience
is an un-breathable sphere.

Only electricity of love
recognizes and cures the sin.

The Forbidden Race

Clocks are concerned
with what
we are not

By racing
the forbidden clocks
we clog them

No Separation

Neither earthquakes
nor volcanoes
Neither floods
nor tornadoes
Neither wars
nor time
can separate us
from our Creator

Mutating Hearts

love cannot change
without a heart

when crowds blindly bow
second thoughts divide
the beats of mutating hearts

the heart cannot change
without love

Terrestrial Love

The soul needs
the healing of attention.
But where there is
a terrestrial love—
there are crutches
and there are feet
that want to stay crippled.

The Exchanged

The exchanged human being
is an abandoned human being—
Applauding such trade
exposes a heart with so many exits
but without a single entrance

The Eyes Of Love

the brakes were
still

i turned away and saw
the deep pearly eyes of love

the next morning
the sunrise began to drift

Opera

Opera is the vocal orchestra
for my pain composition
competing with all instruments.

Indecision

Standing in the doorway
only one side of the door is visible

Hesitation like hinges
needs action

The importance of each decision
impacts millenniums

In The Beginning

uncreated beginnings
are always
a created illusion

in the beginning there was love
love is stronger and older
than even memory or wisdom

being eternal does not mean
life with a helmet
so I remove my armor

Without Any Influence

Sometimes the obscurity of infinity
seems like borders without any influence
where mankind bounces into another mankind
right back in its own backyard
and where its ego echo
steered by the mortal compass
never crosses the cosmic journey

At The Hospital

All cloudless winter
my windows stayed closed,
and the clock was ticking too slowly.
Paper clothes
were hanging on the bedrail
and the door seemed to move
without any hinges.
I had nothing left
except for time and faith.

Evolution

Someday
Something
Will
Become
Someone

No Room

The future has no room
for a faulty victory

The end always serves
the beginning

The Homeless

Where do you go
if you cannot afford
even the street life?

The Recollections

Do not collect
all the memories—
but only those
that both
want to be remembered
and are worthy.

The Stain

Nothing can stop my laughter
when I am picked up
by the very stain I scrubbed
and I get stirred along
with the soap bubbles
in the sink

Irresistible

A hummingbird
is fluttering
right in front of my nose
and tries to distract me,
but wild strawberries are ripe
and today
they cannot hide
from my taste.

The Slave

Space breathes in me.
I find myself
under a pillow
or a command.
I try to hide
but nothing's left of me—
even hidden.
For I am a slave.

Captive Audience

The cold
has captured
a stream

The Ultimate Betrayal

The ultimate mask
always greets us with a kiss

Executive Decision

We should love our enemies—
but not protect them

The Inspection

Polyester emotions
grade the cotton field feelings

Disconnected

Expensive news
follows our cheap work

Recollection With An Attitude

Each time
we want to change the past
we corrupt history

A Short Acquaintance

As I try to greet you
I trip over my long skirt

Apathy

From a blank letter in an envelope
even a callus feels a paper cut.

I understood the empty message—
I smelled it.

But the sight
ignored the smell.

Thirst

The measurement for thirst
is rough
only if somebody else
is thirsty

Paupers

After the last breath we take—
our worn-out boots are finally exchanged
for polished dress shoes

Invasion

You invade
by proving that everyone is weak

You puncture
each breath we take alone

When we use your crutches
we are always brittle like docile gems

A Reminder

The heart
can
break

A Distraction

When shadows are forced
to stay on the ground
even a gopher can ruin
a divine experience

Birds Of Prey

Sometimes
even fragrant moments are disliked.
In the smallest basket—
birds of prey

In the barn
the hay gets too warm
for infinity
to prove its meaning

The Search

There is one universe
in the whole creation
that just seems at first
to make no sense . . .

Because it takes all of us
to search for the Creator,
yet it takes each of us
to find Him . . .

Potential For Darkness

Harmoniously
born soul
is the expression of joy.

Yet within the circumference
of measuring and evaluation
there is a potential for darkness.

Relationships

Soul is like a monarch without a crown
in an endless palace of relationships

Where each mature relationship
is patience

And each immature relationship
is a performance

The Truth

In order
to comprehend the truth—
we need to see the road
it travels

In order
to trust the truth
we need to remove from its road—
the speed limit

Between The Sky Scrapers

Between the sky scrapers
that bump into each other
and grow like fingers of adolescence—
there are piles of garbage
demanding honor.
With so many lights,
but none from within—
everyone feels unneeded.

The Trigger

pride triggers walls
walls trigger fences
fences trigger helmets
helmets trigger bullets
bullets trigger bombs—
bombs strip the pride

The Reservation

You reserved
your trip to heaven
yesterday

You pay
for it
today

Compassion

do not repair,
do not scorn
and do not wipe my tears

just taste them
and they will dry up
on their own

Panoramic Imagination

Thoughts
without wings
are words
without inspiration.
The panoramic imagination
is always beautiful
in the eyes that are open
and focused
and in the eyes
that keep promises

Cursed

Do not punish
a rash and careless blame.
It is already cursed.

Independence

Each time
we leave home—
it is easier
to close the door behind.

The Fear

I close myself in a safe
holding the contents
of my life

The Fences

The fences
always
trespass

One Breath At A Time

Between our toughest fights
there's a compulsive forgiveness
which releases others
from our revengeful attention
one breath at a time.

The Insanity Circle

The minds
are charging us
for thinking

The hearts
are paying us
for feeling

*   *   *

*"Keep on building rock castles
until you know others . . .
Keep on building sand castles
until you know yourself . . ."*

Akiane

Part VII

The Photo Album

The fifth birthday

Bored with coloring books during her kindergarten class, five-year-old Akiane succeeds in convincing her family to take her out of school.

The Photo Album

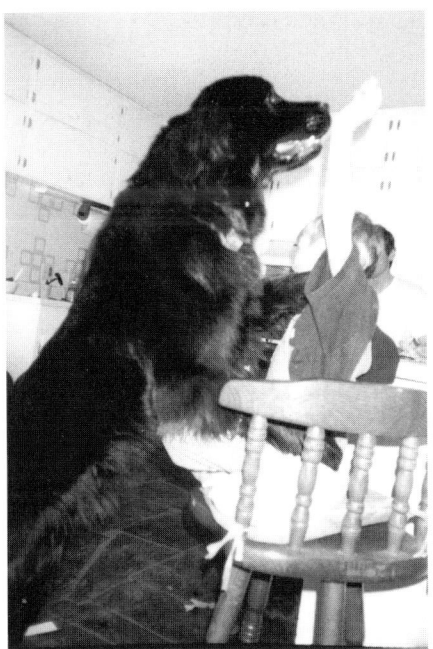

Family dog Meshke outgrowing the kitchen.

Six-year-old Akiane is playing with brother Jeanlu. The poem "The Birdfeeder" is based on their close relationship.

Six-year-old Akiane at a parochial school. "The only thing I liked there was prayer time and breaks for human interaction."

Six-year-old Akiane is fascinated with a home birth of her third brother, eleven-pound newborn Ilia

The Photo Album

Akiane, age 7, during her first months of writing

Seven-and-a–half-year-old home-schooled Akiane loves spending more time outdoors.

My Dream Is Bigger Than I

Akiane, age 8, painting a portrait of Jesus: "Prince of Peace–the Resurrection". The Poem "Stolen Painting" had been written a month before.

Akiane, age 8, during her first interview

The Photo Album

Eight-year-old Akiane in her backyard

Akiane, age 8

Next to her art, nine-year-old Akiane is reading a poem

Reading poetry

The Photo Album

Nine-year-old Akiane reciting poetry during her first solo art exhibition.

Nine-year-old Akiane is playing with a baby from Madagascar.

My Dream Is Bigger Than I

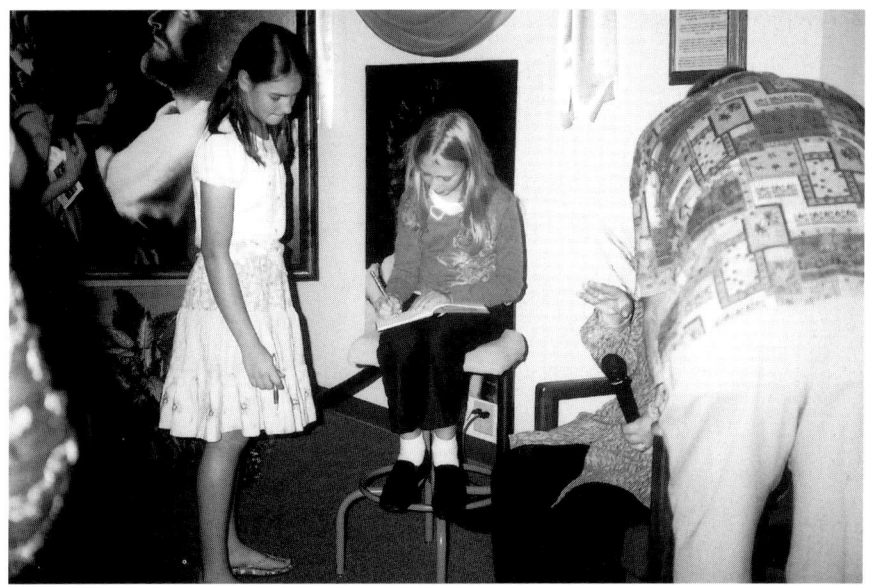

Ten-year-old Akiane reciting poetry and autographing for a large crowd waiting in line during her first museum exhibit

Autographs, autographs and more autographs...Akiane enjoyed autographing with two or three different color pens at the same time.

The Photo Album

Akiane, age 10, shows her three year-old brother Ilia how she paints. This is the only time she allowed anyone to touch her canvas. "The Extraction Of Inspiration" is the poem inspired by this moment.

Reciting poetry during a radio show

Ten-year-old Akiane is painting at her studio. Meeting a girl who had been abandoned was an inspiration behind the commissioned painting "Hope" dedicated to the Listen campaign and auctioned off at Christies auction house in New York to help 200 charities around the world.

During the television show

The Photo Album

Akiane, age 10, during another solo art exhibit, reading poetry and answering questions from reporters, schoolchildren, and philanthropists.

Akiane in the studio for Bob&Sheri national radio show

Ten-year-old Akiane during a television show with other child prodigies

Akiane, age 11, in her studio painting her self-portrait "Co-creation"

The Photo Album

Eleven-year old Akiane finishes her painting, "Love At First Sight"

Eleven-year-old Akiane rocking with her tea-cup poodle KoKo

For more information
about Akiane and her art,
please visit:

www.artakiane.com

To contact Akiane studio gallery
and Akiane, please write
by E-mail to:

love@artakiane.com

or by postal mail to:
**Artakiane LLC
PO BOX 2860
Post Falls ID 83877**

To place orders for Akiane's other books and art, or to inquire
about participation in Akiane's ministry, please call:

1-800-318-0947

The Photo Album

Akiane's first book

Akiane's self-portrait, *Co-Creation*, acrylic, age 11, 48 x 60